Lad Power!

They're Five guys from Britain—Abs, J, Ritchie, Scott, and Sean—who are invading U.S. airwaves with their unique mix of pop, hip-hop, funk, and rap! Find out how these young lads were brought together . . . what life is like in the house they share . . . and what influences helped produce their fresh, danceable grooves.

What was life like for the boys in Five, growing up in different parts of the U.K.? What makes them different from other boy groups on the pop music scene? Which of the Five would be the perfect boyfriend for you? Read all the dish on your favorite Five-some, then quiz yourself and your friends to see who's the biggest fan of . . .

Look for these celebrity biographies from Archway Paperbacks

Backstreet Boys ★ Aaron Carter by Matt Netter
Five by Matt Netter
Hanson: MMMBop to the Top by Jill Matthews
Isaac Hanson: Totally Ike! by Nancy Krulik
Taylor Hanson: Totally Taylor! by Nancy Krulik
Zac Hanson: Totally Zac! by Matt Netter
Hanson: The Ultimate Trivia Book! by Matt Netter
Jewel: Pieces of a Dream by Kristen Kemp
Jonathan Taylor Thomas: Totally JTT! by Michael-Anne Johns
Leonardo DiCaprio: A Biography by Nancy Krulik
Pop Quiz: Leonardo DiCaprio by Nancy Krulik
Matt Damon: A Biography by Maxine Diamond with Harriet
 Hemmings
Most Wanted: Holiday Hunks
'N Sync: Tearin' Up the Charts by Matt Netter
Pop Quiz by Nancy Krulik
Prince William: The Boy Who Will Be King by Randi Reisfeld
Will Power!: A Biography of Will Smith by Jan Berenson

For orders other than by individual consumers, Pocket
Books grants a discount on the purchase of 10 or more
copies of single titles for special markets or premium use.
For further details, please write to the Vice-President of
Special Markets, Pocket Books, 1633 Broadway, New
York, NY 10019-6785, 8th Floor.

For information on how individual consumers can place
orders, please write to Mail Order Department, Simon &
Schuster Inc., 200 Old Tappan Road, Old Tappan, NJ
07675.

Five

An Unauthorized Biography

Matt Netter

AN ARCHWAY PAPERBACK
Published by POCKET BOOKS
New York   London   Toronto   Sydney   Tokyo   Singapore

AN ARCHWAY PAPERBACK *Original*

An Archway Paperback published by
POCKET BOOKS, a division of Simon & Schuster Inc
1230 Avenue of the Americas, New York, NY 10020

Copyright © 1999 by Matt Netter

ISBN: 0-671-03639-4

First Archway Paperback printing Februrary 1999

10 9 8 7 6 5 4 3 2 1

AN ARCHWAY PAPERBACK and colophon are registered trademarks of Simon & Schuster Inc.

Front cover photo by Bernhard Kuhmstedt/Retna ©1998.
Back cover photo by Denis Van Tine/London Features ©1998.

Printed in the U.S.A.

IL 4+

To Me-ma, the toughest old bird I know and definitely the coolest grandma in town.

contents

contents

xi

Five

introduction

They're the hottest group to come out of Great Britain since the Spice Girls. They've got a fresh, new sound—a mixture of pop, hip hop, funk, and rap over a thick layer of unstoppable beats and stirred up with polished harmonies. They're not just another group of young male singers. They are songwriters, dancers, and spectacular performers. They are J, Abs, Rich, Sean, and Scott, and together they are Five— five guys who are serious about their music, but know very well how to have fun; five guys handsome enough to each star on his own TV show; and five guys who each have a look and personality all his own, with attitude to spare. Five has taken Europe by storm and now they've set their sights on America.

When they first came on the pop music scene in the summer of 1997, Five had an identity crisis. Some music fans confused them with another group called Take 5, and others felt there wasn't room for another boy band on the radio. However, it didn't take very long for Five to prove themselves. Within a few short months, all of Great Britain was hooked on their first single, "Slam Dunk (Da Funk)" and the rest of Europe quickly followed suit.

Five introduced themselves to music fans through their videos, performances, and a wave of publicity and promotion. By the end of the year, half the world knew who Five was and had fallen in love with the talents, looks, and yes, attitudes, of Abs Breen, 19, Ritchie Neville, 19, J Brown, 22, Sean Conlon, 18, and Scott Robinson, 19.

Five is not your typical pop group and they are quick to tell anyone who'll listen that they're as different from the Backstreet Boys, Boyzone, and 'N Sync as Hanson is from Wu Tang Clan. They write their own music, their songs don't all sound alike, they don't wear matching outfits, and they're not afraid to say what's on their minds. They're British, they're brash, and they're brazen, but they are not a boy band.

One thing Five definitely is, is misunderstood. They're not an angry group. They hold nothing against anyone. They feel that every band has its place, and theirs is at the top doing what they love to do—writing songs, recording music, and performing for their fans. Their self-titled debut album has been a hit machine, so far churning out three chart toppers in the United States and six overseas.

"When The Lights Go Out" was a monster hit overseas, and when it was later released in America in 1998, it became one of the biggest hits of the summer. Several more hits followed, including "Got The Feelin'," "It's The Things You Do," and "Until The Time Is Through." What put them over the top though, was the song that hit number one, led to an award-winning video, and proved to be Five's anthem—"Everybody Get Up."

By the close of 1998, Five had taken over the pop charts and won the hearts of girls all over America. By the start of 1999, J, Abs, Sean, Scott, and Ritchie had reached the very peak of pop music. They'd left their mark on radio stations, video music channels, record stores, concert arenas, and teen bedroom walls all over the planet. The coming year has plenty more excitement in store for the cheeky quintet, but, true to their characters, Five is ready for anything.

How did these five characters all manage to gravitate toward one another? Do they all get along as friends? What goes on inside the house they all live in together? Which rumors about them are true? What are Ritchie, Sean, Abs, Scott, and J each really like? How on earth did a brand-new band manage to put together such a sensational debut album? What's the story behind their videos and performances? What's it like touring the world and how do they handle the overwhelming attention from fans at every stop? What lies ahead for Five? All of these questions and many more are answered in *Five*.

1
round up the lads

In early 1997, an ad was placed in a British newspaper that caught the attention of young aspiring
musicians throughout the country. It read something like, "Five lads needed for a new pop band.
Audition to be held in London." The ad was
placed by the father and son music management
team of Bob and Chris Herbert, famous for having launched the Spice Girls a few years earlier
through a similar tactic. "With everything we
learned from the Spice Girls," Chris said in
Faces in Pop magazine, "we wanted to bring
together a new boy act, but not the usual crop of
boy bands. We wanted a band with attitude and
edge. As soon as we saw these five guys, we knew
they had it, both musically and character wise."

Those five fresh faces and voices were then
singer/rapper/deejay Richard "Abs" Breen, 17,
from nearby Enfield; Scott Robinson, 17, a smart

alec soprano singer from Essex; Richard Neville, 17, a Birmingham singer with matinee idol looks; Jason "J" Brown, a tough looking 20-year-old singer/rapper/producer from the south England military town Aldershot; and a precocious crooner from Leeds named Sean Conlon, 15.

The Birth Of Five

The guys will never forget the day they met. "There was a talent search held around the country in England," Scott recalled in a press conference with some American teen magazines. "There were about three thousand people at the first audition and at the second audition, it got rounded down to fourteen boys." By then, the five lads had gotten to know each other.

"We all got on at that point," J recalled. "We got to talking and we sort of found out we had some bits in common. When we met some of the other guys, they were like, 'Oh, yeah, I'm going to do this because I saw that thing in the paper and I decided to go for it.'"

"It's not like that for all of us," Rich pointed

out. "We've all, from a very early age, wanted to do this."

"When we got to the last audition there were nine other boys," Scott added, "and basically, we said to them, 'We want to go forward as five.'" Individually, Scott, Rich, J, Abs, and Sean were like lightning in a bottle. Together, as five, they were a thunderstorm of energy, desire, and immense talent. Chris and Bob took immediate notice and signed the guys on under their management company, Safe Management.

"It was so amazing when it happened," Scott recalled in *Teen Beat* magazine. "But, it was really weird because there was meant to be four or five more auditions afterward, but then, obviously, it went through. So, basically, we got there on that day and then it all happened really quickly." With their reputation, and the guys' talents, it took Bob and Chris no time at all to land them a recording contract with RCA Records and then hook them up with choreographer Paul Domaine and producer Denniz Pop.

In the very short time they had together, before "getting thrown into the deep end" as J put it, the guys had a few things to work out. First, to avoid any confusion between the two Riches, Richard Breen began going by a nickname, Abs, which is not because he's proud of his washboard stomach muscles, but because it is short for his middle name, Abidin. Richard Neville would continue to go by Rich or Ritchie.

The next order of business was to come up with a name for themselves. They had very little time to be creative and they knew they didn't want a name as complicated as Prophets of Da Funk, J's previous band, or as vulgar as Anal Beard, Ritchie's previous band. Hmmm. Let's see, five lads, five different voices and looks. Why not Five? It's simple enough. But, is it "Five," "5," or "5ive"? "How should you write it? Any way you want to, mate," Abs explained in *Smash Hits*. "You do what you want."

Off The Deep End

From the day they signed on with their management to the day you're reading this, it has been a non-stop ride of recording, rehearsing, performing, promotion, publicity, and loads and loads of flying for Five. Like the Spice Girls before them, Five was immediately thrown into a house together so they could bond as friends as well as band mates. After all, if they were to do that much traveling together, they'd better get to know one another. But, that too would have to wait.

"There are lots of things that bands have to decide on," J told *16* magazine. "But, we moved into our house there on May tenth [1997], and then on May eleventh, the next day, we went to Sweden and recorded." Five flew to Stockholm, Sweden, to meet up with their producer, Denniz Pop, as well as several other prominent producers and song writers at Cheiron Studios.

The Five guys unpacked their bags and got settled in Stockholm because they would be spending the next two months there recording songs for their debut CD. They spent long days in the studio, writing music and singing, while the production team polished their work to a shine. What kind of sound had Five achieved? "We're doing pop music," J told *Tiger Beat* magazine. "We're not just doing ballads and things with our music. We add different things like rap, but we're not a hip-hop band. We're still a pop band."

Five came away from the Sweden recording session with six tracks, "Everybody Get Up," "My Song," "Until The Time Is Through," "Partyline 555-On-Line," "It's The Things You Do," and "Slam Dunk (Da Funk)," which would serve as their first single. The remaining tracks were later recorded in other European studios with different producers.

That August, the guys found themselves back in England ready to introduce themselves to the pop scene as Five for the first time. "The very first thing we did was perform for Radio 1," J recalled in *All-Stars* magazine. "It was the first time we performed as a band and we were supposed to do a warm-up act to get the crowd going before we went live on the air. We went on to do the warm-up and the deejay came over and said, 'The crowd has gotten so crazy over you that we want to put you live on the air.' We go on stage and there are all these people going absolutely ballistic. I didn't know what to expect!" Welcome to stardom, Five.

Room For One More

No matter how many pop acts there are, when you're as talented and appealing as Five, there's always room for more. Even *Billboard* magazine, the music industry bible, couldn't help but agree. In an early review of Five, an article read, "Does pop radio need yet another clique of young, videogenic harmonizers? The answer was a resounding no . . . until the onset of Five, a U.K. quintet of cuties who swagger with undeniably sharp vocal precision and an appealing degree of soul. Five are the first real reason the Backstreet Boys have had to look over their shoulders in a serious sweat."

For the Five guys, it's not about competition at all. "We're not trying to compete with any of the bands that have come before," Scott explained in *Faces in Pop* magazine. "We're just making the music we love. We know that there have been quite a few bands that have come along over the last few years who apparently share the same influences that we do, but that's fine. We respect them—and hopefully, before long, they'll respect us as well."

Five isn't at all like other pop bands and they don't like comparisons. "We're a lad band, not a boy band," Sean has explained again and again. "You see, you get your boys, and then you get your lads—like us." In England, a "lad" is a young man, more mature than a boy, but not as conservative as a man. The term is used like "guy" in America—an everyday Joe who plays sports, likes girls, and sticks by his friends.

Five stick by each other and they also stick to what they believe in and who they are. "We haven't got a message like [the Backstreet Boys]," Scott told Australia's *TV Hits* magazine. "We just wanna do our own thing. We don't get told what to wear and say, you know?"

"Boy bands wear all matching clothes and frilly shirts and that's not us," Sean added. No, Five has a style all their own. They each wear what they're comfortable in and what suits their individual tastes.

They're not the Spice Girls either, as J pointed out. "There are no gimmicks with us. It's not like we're going to go on about 'Lad Power!' We're just trying to make music and do our thing. We don't want to change the world."

For Five, it's all about the music and the fans, as J explained in *Faces in Pop* magazine. "All we can ask is that people listen to what we do. We hope they like it. That's our primary ambition—to make music that people all around the world can listen to and enjoy."

Let's Get This Party Started

Shortly after the Radio 1 event, Five was back at their flat in Surrey watching television, not aware that the moment of their arrival was about to happen. "We just sat there watching TV," Ritchie recalled in *Bop* magazine, "and all of a sudden the ['Slam Dunk (Da Funk)'] video came on. We were like, 'Who's that? Oh, my God!' We were really excited."

"It was all so new to us," Scott added. "We were jumping up and down on the sofa and stuff, going, 'I don't believe it!'" Well, keep jumping Scott, because it's all up hill from here.

2

everybody get up

Slam Dunk (Da Funk) got serious radio play, and in November, when it was released as a single, it cracked the top ten on the British pop charts. Five was making themselves known, and through word of mouth, a series of local performances drew quite a crowd. "Word spread because we were doing a small tour for like a week," Ritchie told *Superstars* magazine.

"Some people traveled to see us at one point and then went four or five hours in the car, a couple of hundred miles, to go to the next one," J added. Word would travel much further as Five's record company began getting bombarded with media requests for interviews and photo shoots. The teen press tripped over each other to get to Five. The guys posed for hundreds of pictures and answered thousands of questions from the overseas teen press. *Big!*, *Bliss*, *J-17*,

Live & Kicking, Sugar, TV Hits, Top of the Pops, and *Smash Hits* all wanted a piece of Five.

Pleased To Meet You?

The press couldn't possibly have prepared themselves for Five. "When we first came out, we took some getting used to," J explained to *Tiger Beat* magazine. "At first everybody was saying, 'Oh, Five, they've got attitudes.' It's because we don't act false toward anybody and we speak our minds. Once they pick up on it, then they start to like us."

"Maybe it's because they're used to the way a lot of other bands are," Abs suggested. "I don't think kids can relate to a band that says they never have girlfriends, always rehearse, and never stay out late. I think they know it's not true."

"What a lot of bands say is like scripted," J added. "With us, we say what we really feel and it's like a normal conversation. If one of us has a girlfriend, we'll admit it. A lot of press—teen press and even tabloids—tell us they enjoy interviewing us." And, in turn, millions of young fans have enjoyed reading about Five in those magazines.

Flyin' High

At the end of 1997, Five participated in the annual *Smash Hits* tour. Even with established groups like Boyzone and Backstreet Boys onboard, the brand-new Five didn't get lost in the shuffle. In fact, *Smash Hits* readers voted them the Best New Tour Group of 1997. This was a huge break for Five, and word spread further about them. Five kicked off 1998 by zipping around the globe to promote their album. They did radio interviews and made major record store appearances all over Europe, as well as in Asia and Australia. It was overwhelming and exhausting.

J went on a bit about Five's lack of sleep in *Superteen* magazine. "Well, it's like this for most bands, but we just don't go to bed. On the *Smash Hits* tour, we only got something like eight hours sleep for the week's tour. We just go on autopilot. It's another level, it's not like you're too tired to perform. Once you've gone a certain amount of time without any sleep, you go onto a totally different level and wavelength, and you can work that way." Scott added, "I can't do it that often, but, when I do, I enjoy it." Come on, Scott, stay awake. There's plenty more where that came from.

In March, Five's second single, "When The Lights Go Out," was released in Europe. As the song climbed the charts all the way to number four, it got tremendous radio play and thousands of video requests en route to going gold. "All over the world we're getting massive," Scott said in *Big!* magazine. "It's really weird."

Five packed their things (again) and headed to America where they were ready to make some noise. "When The Lights Go Out" was the first Five single released in the United States. To promote it, the guys did a weeklong publicity tour. "We've flown out here for just eight days," J told *16* magazine. "Before that it was Belgium, Holland, Greece, Sweden. We really don't get to stay put for long."

They met with magazines and radio stations in New York and Los Angeles. "New York's cool 'cause there's loads of shops and stuff, and L.A. I like a lot," Abs told *Teen Beat* magazine.

"I didn't like New York much," Ritchie added. "It's too busy, too much like London. I liked L.A. because of the sun."

"I can see Rich packing up and leaving the band to become a surf dude," Scott joked. "He loves the beach. He's a total sun freak!"

Upon returning to England, Five released their third single, "Got The Feelin'," filmed some videos, and made the startling realization that they had become celebrities. "Because we're out of the country a lot, and every time we go back, we forget how big we are in Britain, Europe as well," J told *All-Stars* magazine. "We go into the streets now and people are taking pictures of us and chasing after us. It's just all blown up. We're like the biggest pop band in Britain."

If this level of success seemed to happen overnight for Five, it's because it practically did. "What other bands took two years to do, we did in four months," J told *Tiger Beat* magazine.

Sean has a theory on why it happened so quickly. "Other bands concentrate on one area. Like, the Backstreet Boys stayed in Germany for about a year before they came to America. We didn't leave England to do Europe and we're not leaving Europe to do America. We don't stay anywhere for longer than three days."

Out Of Sight

The guys in Five love making videos. And based on how often their videos are requested on MTV, Much Music, and The Box, their fans love to watch them. "Videos are really fun to do," Scott gloated in *Bop* magazine. But they are also a lot of work as Ritchie pointed out. "People say to you it's hard work and you're going to get really tired," Ritchie explained in *Bop* magazine. "I have reached new levels of tiredness in this band."

As is the case with their music, Five has plenty of say when it comes to filming videos. For instance, did you know that the "When The

Lights Go Out" video was originally scripted to be a lot sexier? The guys didn't feel comfortable with it, however, and had it toned down. "There was one part in the American version of 'When The Lights Go Out' when it was supposed to be like this fabric hanging down, and a fan was supposed to blow it against our bodies so it sort of clung to you," J explained in *Bop* magazine. "But, straightaway, we said to everybody that we don't do that kind of thing. So, that got taken out of the script."

It's very important to the Five guys how they are portrayed to their fans. "You always think, 'the way I acted on TV, that isn't actually how I act,'" J said. "But that's how everybody else is going to see me."

"I think, 'Is that really how people see me?'" Sean added. In the video for "Everybody Get Up" there is no need for the Fivesters to worry about their appearances. Together with their management and record company, Five sensed that their fourth single was going to be a smash. They were all right. The single debuted at number two on the U.K. charts and the video put it over the top.

A smash hit needs a killer video, so a team of talented directors was brought in to make the now historic video for "Everybody Get Up." Shot in downtown London, the video makes Sean, J, Abs, Ritchie, and Scott appear larger than life. Since the American video might differ from the original European version, which, by the way, went on to win awards, here's the gist of it.

In an English prep school, a large classroom full of students takes instruction from a stuffy, old professor prior to an exam. The professor gets paged to the headmaster's office and says he will be back in five minutes. Students begin to bang their rulers on their desks in unison and, as if summoned from a more perfect existence, out struts Five. Clad in leather jackets, Sean, Scott, J, Abs, and Ritchie make their way toward the classroom in slow motion. On their way, Abs shuts off the lights and the electric beginning of "Everybody Gets Up" begins with the explosive guitar riff and J's sinister laugh.

The madness of Five takes over the classroom and the exam turns into an all-out party. Everyone gets up out of their seats and begins dancing and doing gymnastics while Five perform up in front of the classroom. Five kicks it up another notch as Rich and Scott splatter buckets of paint all over everyone, and the room transforms into a Woodstock-like concert. The sprinklers are set off and it is raining indoors while Abs and Sean run through the crowd and J body surfs over it. As the song ends, a dumbfounded professor returns. He turns the lights back on and wonders what on earth happened as five lads in leather walk off behind him.

"That was real paint—everyone got messed up," Abs told *Teen Beat* magazine. "Oh yeah, it was one of the best videos we've made. We really enjoyed making it and it turned out fantastic."

Five: Inside

"We're making a long form video," J explained to *Smash Hits* magazine. "The idea is we all do something that suits our personalities." The home video, filmed all over England, came out in November 1998. According to Five's official website, "It features never seen before, especially recorded, exclusive footage on Five. It is a close up on the lives of the lads and sees them talking openly about the things they enjoy, life in the band, their views on each other as well as some serious sporting action." *Five: Inside* also includes all of Five's videos. Included are "Slam Dunk (Da Funk)," "Everybody Get Up," "Got The Feelin'," "Until The Time Is Through," and both the U.S. and European versions of "When The Lights Go Out."

For the sporting action, each band member had a camera crew follow him around for a day while he took part in an activity. "I'm racing cars, Rich's playing [soccer], Sean's playing rugby, and Scott's playing basketball," Abs told *Teen Beat* magazine. "J's jumping out of a plane."

"I did my first ten thousand foot skydive," J added. "I had to do it tandem because I'd never done it, but I'm going to keep on until I can do it on my own." J went skydiving with the London Parachute School in Oxfordshire. For the jump he did, an assisted tandem from 10,000 feet, he went up in a tiny plane, circled for a half hour, and then jumped. His buddy

Sean watched from the ground. J wanted to do it again right away, but Heathrow Flight Central wouldn't allow it.

Abs spent his day at the Brands Hatch racetrack. To get the hang of it, Abs drove six laps around the track with an instructor in a BMW. After that, the daredevil hopped in a single seater Formula One racing car and zipped around solo for ten laps. The other three guys weren't quite so daring.

Sean visited the London Bronco's training ground to take part in his favorite sport, rugby. He's been a player and fan since he was a kid. Sean took part in a training session with the team. The players and coaches liked Sean and asked him to come back soon to watch a game. Before leaving, Sean got his photo taken with the whole team.

Scott had company during his day of fun. Three hundred fans were invited to the filming as Scott visited the London Leopards, his local basketball team. After a bit of training, Scott played in an exhibition game with the pros and then got his picture taken with the team as well as the mayor of South End. After the game, the basketball players played a little joke on Scott and yanked his shorts down! But, that didn't faze Scott one bit, as he later returned to watch a real game, only he didn't get to see much, as he spent the entire time signing autographs for fans.

For Ritchie's day in the sun, he headed home to visit his family in Birmingham and let the camera crew get a sense of his childhood. Ever since he was a kid, Ritchie has rooted for the Aston Villa soccer team. Lucky Rich got to get a tour of their team facilities from his favorite player Peter Withe. Peter, a former star player who is now a talent scout, took Ritchie out on the practice field for some one-on-one training. This photo op yielded a picture Ritchie will treasure for years to come. Afterward, he and the camera crew dropped by the pub his mom owns for a cold drink.

R & R

After over a year of constant traveling to record their album, promote it all over the world, grant interviews and photo shoots, and perform concerts, without nearly enough sleep or time with their families, the Five guys needed a break. "We had a couple of weeks off," Abs told *Teen Beat* magazine. "Up until then, we'd gone nonstop. We'd fly here, fly there, and do interviews and such."

"A lot of the time, when we're seen or heard moaning it's because we're so tired," J explained in *Smash Hits* magazine. "We're okay at the moment 'cause we've all just had a holiday, but when you're knackered [Brit speak for exhausted], everything gets you wound up and I think a lot of people catch us in that mood."

Typical to their nature, the Five guys each had their own individual ways of finding relaxation in all corners of the globe. J and Sean spent time in the Greek Islands, Ritchie went to Thailand with his family, Scott and his family went to Disney World in Florida, and Abs swept his girlfriend off to Barbados in the Caribbean. "It was really nice, really beautiful," Abs told *Smash Hits* magazine.

Of course, their relaxation was interrupted a

few times. After all, no matter how far a pop star travels, he's bound to be spotted by fans. "There were a few English people who recognized me," Scott told *Smash Hits* magazine. "They were looking at me a bit funny, as if to say, 'Is that Scott from Five?' But my mom and dad were calling me Dan for the whole holiday to throw people off the scent."

There was no fooling Ritchie's fans however. Even in Thailand the gorgeous guy couldn't escape his adoring fans. "There were a couple of girls at [the hotel] reception when I was signing in, and they came up and said, 'You're Rich from Five, aren't you?'" he recalled. "I was like, 'Yeah,' but it was okay, there were no problems."

Fan Frenzy

Beyond the realm of the typical fan there are the truly insane. "We've got what we call 'hard-core fans,'" Scott told *Superteen* magazine. "They're the nutcase ones that are there every day wherever we are. They expect us to know their names and they touch our bums!"

"Before we got in a band, we didn't realize you get fans who stay with you," J told *All-Stars* magazine. "We have girls who wait for us at airports at two in the morning. They found out where we were living and they'd come to our house at one in the morning. Some turn up at odd places."

"When we left to fly to America, they were at the airport and said, 'See you when you get back!'" Scott added. "I actually have asked fans where I'm to be next because some of them seem to know our schedule better than I do. English fans are mental."

"They know things about us that we don't even know about us," Ritchie added. "It's kind of scary." Especially when you consider the guys also get packages delivered to their house from strange people. Usually it's just candy or a teddy bear from a fan, but you never know. Ritchie says fans sometimes send them sneakers or T-shirts and somehow know all their sizes!

"Some of our fans go to extremes," Abs told *Teen Beat* magazine. "They'll sleep outside our hotel for like three nights in a row."

Even the most extreme fan frenzies don't rile Sean though. "We count ourselves quite lucky and we just go along and have a good laugh," he added.

3

splendid songs

"We have so much control about what goes on the album," J told *Bop* magazine. "The contract that we got drawn up with our management [reads as] more of a partnership. They're not our bosses." Considering that J had prior experience with producing and arranging, Abs was an accomplished deejay, and both were keen rappers, there was a lot of group creativity at Five's disposal. Together with Sean's smooth R & B voice and the tender soprano pipes of Scott and Ritchie, J and Abs would work with a battery of song writers and producers to create a groundbreaking record.

A Delicious Debut

"We wanted each track to be thought of as a hit," Abs explained to *Bop* magazine. "So, when you play the album, each track is sort of literally a hit." To help them achieve this lofty goal, Five's record company, RCA, enlisted the guidance and creative talents of Denniz Pop and Max Martin, a renowned writing/producing tandem that had previously developed hit songs for Backstreet Boys, 'N Sync, Robyn, Ace of Base, and 3T. Pop and Martin were behind half of the songs on *Five*, including four of the six singles. The Pop/Martin tracks were all recorded at the famous Cheiron Studios in Stockholm, Sweden.

The remaining tracks were produced, arranged, and recorded at eight different studio locations throughout Europe by more than a dozen other dance music mavens, including Eliot Kennedy (Spice Girls, Take That), Herb Crichlow (Backstreet Boys), Kristian Lundin ('N Sync, Backstreet Boys), Richard "Biff" Stannard (Spice Girls, East 17), and Cutfather and Joe (Mark Morrison, Peter Andre). With so many artists in the background and the talented Five in the foreground, the resulting recording is a flawless album with a wide range of sounds, including harmonies, changing leads, and rap backed by infectious beats and hooks.

"You know when you buy an album and you listen to it and all the tracks are the same?" Sean pointed out in *Bop* magazine. "It's not like that. It's just different styles all the way through. All of it is pop music with different styles."

"Basically, it's seventy different sounds," Scott added. "We haven't got that many slow tracks on the album. [There's] a couple of slow tracks, but they're like ballads with a bit of an edge, instead of just something to make the girls cry." Many bands that have been around for years never put out an album as polished and thoroughly solid as Five did with their very first recording.

Industry experts were extremely impressed with the freshman effort from Five. *Music Boulevard*, one of the premier music sites on the Internet, tabbed the album "A magic blend of smooth rap, R & B flava, rock, and romance." Five was able to achieve exactly what they aimed for with their debut record partly because they had so much to do with it.

Unlike most other modern day pop bands, Five has a hand in creating the songs they sing.

In fact, Ritchie, Sean, J, Abs, and Scott co-wrote eight of the twelve songs on *Five*. "We've co-written virtually every track on the album," J told *Tiger Beat* magazine. "So, we want people to sort of know that we're not just totally manufactured things that just go on stage, and that we really are into our music." One listen to *Five*, and that becomes very obvious.

Following is a breakdown of Five's self-titled debut CD, including studio details, background information, and song interpretations. Songs marked with a "°" were released as singles.

FIVE

"When The Lights Go Out"°
Billboard magazine raved about the single, saying, "'When The Lights Go Out' chugs with faux-funk authority and a crackling pop chorus. You will be irreversibly hooked on this tasty guilty pleasure long before the track reaches its conclusion." Based on the incredible success the single achieved both in Europe and in America, music fans agreed.

This racy love song about a guy trying to win over a girl made the perfect first single for the American market. It spent nearly the entire summer of 1998 in the *Billboard* Top 10. In Europe, it served as the second single off the album and reached as high as number four on the U.K. pop charts. The "When The Lights Go Out" video has the lads in a bowling alley, dancing on the lanes while Abs does the deejaying.

"When The Lights Go Out" combines Five's fluid vocals with a funk beat and the keyboard melodies of Joe Belmaati. The guys alternate singing with Sean singing the verses and the guys alternating during the chorus. Abs adds a hot bit of rap to mix things up. The single was co-written by Five with Eliot Kennedy, Tim Lever, and Mike Percy, who produced it. Cutfather and Joe with Mads Nilsson mixed and recorded the song at Medley Studio.

"That's What You Told Me"

Many of the same players who created "When The Lights Go Out" were also onboard for the recording of "That's What You Told Me." Cutfather and Joe produced, mixed, and recorded the track with Nilsson at C&J Studio and Medley Studio. Five co-wrote "That's What You Told Me" with Joe Belmaati and others. Joe again provided the keyboards, while Aliway provided the background vocals.

The song is about a girl who takes a relationship for granted and a guy who tells her how hurt he is. "That's What You Told Me" is a potent urban pop track that showcases the individual talents of every guy in the group. Alternating upbeat harmonies are intermingled with a hard hitting chorus and bitter rap to give the song a heartbreak feel to go with its edgy lyrics.

*"It's The Things You Do"**

America's second single, and likely Europe's sixth, "It's The Things You Do" was steadily climbing the Billboard charts at the time of this writing. This is the type of melody-driven choral-hook single we've all come to expect from Max Martin. After all, Martin also wrote

'N Sync's "I Want You Back" and the Backstreet Boys' "Everybody (Backstreet's Back)." Martin co-wrote "It's The Things You Do" with Herbie Crichlow and Five. Martin also co-produced the track with Jake and makes a cameo on the single, singing backup. Cutfather and Joe with Nilsson were on hand at both Cheiron Studios and Medley Studio for the recording and mixing of the track.

Sean gets to show off his silky voice while J represents with his own brand of power rap in "It's The Things You Do." Ritchie and Scott blend together well in the final chorus, "You've got that Midas touch . . ."

"When I Remember When"

A lot of hard work went into this tender ballad which was produced, mixed, and recorded in three different studios. Cutfather and Joe produced and recorded "When I Remember When" at C&J Studio and Metropolis Studios, while Bernard Lohr mixed the track at Sweet Silence Studios. Sean's solos are backed by Ritchie and Scott's soprano, Bee Gee's style harmonies. Belmaati appears on keyboards and Tue Roth on string arrangement.

Slam Dunk (Da Funk)"

This powerful dose of hip-hop pop launched Five into the music circuit in the fall of 1997. Though it hasn't been released as a single in America, "Slam Dunk (Da Funk)" was a smash in Europe. After a steady rise up the U.K. pop charts, the single topped out at number ten.

"Five bad boys with the power to rock you" is a fitting introduction for a group of take charge musicians new to the scene. All five band members swap vocals in this infectious party song. Ritchie, Sean, and Scott alternate on vocals, while J and Abs bounce raps off each other like the guys do onstage when they perform this song live.

Four different mixes of "Slam Dunk (Da Funk)" were recorded at Cheiron Studios; the Candy Girls Vocal Club Mix, Future Funk, Sol Brothers, and Bug Remix. Martin and Pop wrote and produced the single with help from Jake and Herbie Crichlow. Jair-Rohm Wells plays the thumping bass, while Herbie provides the voice of the commentator. Additional background vocals are provided by Maryth and Nana Hedin.

"Satisfied"

This sensitive soul ditty features some of the best Five harmonies on record. Sean's fluid pipes rotate with the harmonies and J's R & B chatter. J even sings a few bars on this track. Five co-wrote "Satisfied" with T. Hawes and K. Beauvais. Steve Mace produced, arranged, and mixed the track with help from Tim Laws, Dave Walters, and Andy Kowalski. Arden Hart plays keyboards.

"It's All Over"

"It's All Over" is the closest thing Five has to a straight dance track. Five co-wrote this upbeat song that's ironically about a break-up with Eliot Kennedy, Mike Percy, and Tim Lever, who also produced it. Lee McCutcheon and Robin Sellars pitched in for the making of the complicated song that features synthesizers and horns in the background, as well as varying beats and alternating and overlapping voices. Abs does quite a bit of singing on "It's All Over," as do Scott, Ritchie, and Sean, with J adding in a short rap.

"Partyline 555-On-Line"
This bass beat tune about meeting girls at a party was co-written by Five with Crichlow, Pop, and Jake, who also produced it. Ritchie sings quite a bit, as do Scott and Sean, with J doing both singing and rapping with Abs. The background rhythm section in "Partyline" comes from Ingemar Woody on guitar and Tomas Lindberg on bass. Background vocals are courtesy of Jake, Jeanette Soderholm, and Andreas Carlsson.

"Until The Time Is Through"*
This sweet love song spotlights Scott and Ritchie in a beautiful soprano harmony. Hearing and seeing the two gorgeous guys sing "Now and forever, I will be here for you" is enough to melt your heart. During a typical Five perfor-

mance, most of the flowers and teddies get thrown on stage during this song. Martin co-wrote "Until The Time Is Through" with Carlsson, who also provides backing vocals on the album. Belmaati, Roh, and Esbjorn Ohrwall are on background instruments. Martin produced the single with Kristian Lundin at Cheiron Studios. Cutfather and Joe with Nilsson mixed and recorded it at Sweet Silence Studios.

"Until The Time Is Through" was Five's fifth single in Europe, released in November 1998.

*"Everybody Get Up"**

"Everybody Get Up" exploded in Europe and turned into an anthem for Five. It was number one on the British charts and really solidified Five's place in pop music. At the time this book was written, the single was about to be released in America, where there was already a buzz about it. Five loves performing the song live because it sends their crowds into a tizzy. "It's fantastic," Abs told *All-Stars* magazine.

"Whenever we play it—it's our last song—and everyone, even boys who've been sitting down for three or four songs, get up as soon as that track comes on."

"Everybody Get Up" opens with J's sinister laugh and it doesn't let up until the last note—from Abs and J's raps, to the jamming guitar, to the rousing chorus of "Everybody get up, Five will make you get down now." Using a sampling of the rockin' electric guitar (played brilliantly by Per Aldeheim) from Joan Jett's '80s hit "I Love Rock & Roll," the song was written by A. Merrill and J. Hooker and produced by Pop and Jake especially for Five. "Everybody Get Up" was recorded and mixed at Cheiron Studios.

"My Song"
This is as close as Five comes to pure hip-hop. While Sean sings the chorus in between, Abs and J outdo each other with quick-paced raps. It's a fun challenge to try and memorize the verses. Five co-wrote "My Song" with Crichlow, Pop, and Jake, who also produced it. The track was recorded and mixed at Cheiron Studios.

"Got The Feelin'"*

The "na, na, na" song. This PM Dawn style track almost sounds like it came from the West Coast (of the U.S., that is). It's hard to believe a British pop group could write and perform a song like this. J really demonstrates his hip hop prowess on this track and the rest of Five does their best to reel you in with a chorus as catchy as the Spice Girls' "Wannabe." Midway through the song you find yourself bobbing your head up and down muttering, "One if you gonna, two if you wanna, three 'cause everything's all right." J, Sean, and Abs co-wrote "Got the Feelin'" with Julian Gallagher and Biff Stannard.

"Got the Feelin'" was released as Five's third single in Europe in June 1998, around the same time their album debuted in America. A solid follow-up to "Lights," it peaked at number three on the U.K. pop charts.

Bonus tracks on the U.K. version of *Five* include:

"Human"

"Don't You Want It"

"Shake"

"Cold Sweat"

"Straight Up Funk"

If you're a Five fan from the United States or Canada and you must have the version of *Five* containing the additional five tracks, there are two ways you can go about tracking it down. Check the imports section at your local record store. If they don't have it on hand, some stores will special order it for you. If you're online, check the *Music Boulevard* website (www.musicblvd.com). They have the German import version of *Five*, which contains sixteen tracks—the above five and all of the American version except for "When I Remember When."

4

ordinary boys

Since May 1997, J, Abs, Sean, Scott, and Ritchie have lived together in a communal house in the Camberley section of Surrey, a rural, countryside town not too far from London. When you think of five brassy, young musicians sharing a home, what comes to mind? Poetry readings, group picnics, gourmet cuisine. Seriously, though, this is not a normal living situation. Neighbors complain as three different styles of music blast out the windows at late hours, but local schoolgirls don't seem to mind. When they caught on to who resided at that address, they began waiting on the doorstep in groups for the guys to get home. They often leave behind cards, messages, requests, and presents as well.

Band Mates & House Mates

"We're literally five best friends," J told *BB* magazine, but how could that be if these guys hadn't even met prior to their auditions for Five? When they moved into the Surrey house, the Five guys still didn't know each other well. Logically, there was some uncertainty among them as they first became acquainted with one another. Granted they were all British, roughly the same age, and all had musical aspirations. Beyond that there were noticeable differences.

Two band members, J and Scott, were from south of London, while two others, Abs and Sean, were from north and Ritchie was from "somewhere in the middle" as Sean puts it. As far as their demeanors, J and Scott are outspoken, while Ritchie and Sean are more reserved and Abs can go either way depending on his mood. Would these five young guys become fast friends or would their differences have them at each other's throats? "I had no idea what to expect," Sean revealed in *BB* magazine.

The more they got to talking, the more the

five lads realized that they had more than just music in common. "We're all down to earth," Ritchie explained to *Smash Hits* magazine. "We like a good laugh, and that's about it really." This turned out to be a blessing as the Five guys soon laughed off the early awkwardness and any uncertainty was put to rest.

"We hit it off straight away," Scott said in *BB* magazine. "We all just gelled together." When it comes to music, the Five guys are on the same page, with the same drive to be the very best band they can be. Whether they are in the studio, on the road, up on stage, or just at home, it's always a group effort.

"We know each other totally now. We're so close," Ritchie told *BB* magazine. "We're not just band mates. If the band split up today, we know we'd all keep in touch." That doesn't mean the Fivesters don't have their share of disagreements. Ritchie added, "We're together 24 hours a day, seven days a week, so, of course, we have our arguments. But, it's usually over why you left your dirty socks in the living room." Or who's playing their music too loud, who's hogging the phone, who hasn't done their chores, or who's taking too long in the bathroom.

"At the end of the day, we always know we're still friends," Abs added. When a *Teen Beat* magazine reporter asked Abs if he ever gets sick of his band mates, he answered, "I don't ever get sick of them. We get annoyed at each other every now and again. I mean, we work together, we see each other a lot of the time, and we only get a little time off. We know each other very well, and friends argue, but so do couples."

As for young Sean, he's learned a bit about diplomacy as well. "We have our arguments like everyone else," he told *TV Hits* magazine, "but we know we'll be back talking in five minutes."

Nobody has more fun with their little spats than Abs. "If there's an argument, I just sit back," Abs explained. "It seems to wind the others up!"

Tattle Tales

Since the group moved into the house, Sean has had a bedroom to himself. The other guys haven't been so lucky. Abs and Scott share one room, while Rich and J share another. Living in such close quarters has given the guys an opportunity to get to know each other a little too well. They've become accustomed to each other's habits, rituals, and moods.

"I've just discovered I have really big mood swings," Abs told *Teen Machine* magazine. And he's not the only one that this holds true for.

Abs, Sean, Ritchie, and Scott have all had to learn to deal with J's admitted split personality. "I've got my ups and downs," he told *Tiger Beat* magazine. "I might be really right or sometimes I'm really quite moody. I'm never sort of in between. I'm either this good laughing sort and talking a lot, or I just sit there and don't speak at all."

Scott can also be a different person from one moment to the next. "I can be quite moody," Scott told *Superteen* magazine. "I can be really nasty and other times I can be quiet and laid back, but not that often."

Ritchie is the only member of Five who says he doesn't have a temper. The other four have all learned to control theirs since moving in together. "When I first joined the band, I was losing my temper every second, but I realized I couldn't be like that around people, so I calmed myself down a bit," J told *Live & Kicking* magazine.

Getting used to each other's musical taste also took some time. Aside from J, who'll listen to just about anything, the other guys have nearly opposite tastes in music, except that none of them seems to care much for the country and western sound. "If it's good music, I'll listen to anything and enjoy it, but basically, I like hip-hop," J told *Tiger Beat* magazine. "Abs likes R & B and underground dance, Sean likes soul, and Rich is more into Nirvana and things like that. Scott is Mr. Cheesy Pop. He doesn't just like pop, he likes cheesy ballads."

Sleeping habits are also a source of contention. "Abs is really funny in his sleep," Ritchie told *TV Hits* magazine. "The CD player is on the floor by his bed and he taps the lid open and shut in his sleep."

Abs returned the, uh, compliment. "Rich is weird. He has nervous twitches and snores all the time!" As far as sleeping times are concerned, Abs and Scott go to bed the earliest and Sean and Scott are usually the last to wake up. J, the grandpa of the group, often takes on the responsibility of making sure everybody gets up, no pun intended. "Sometimes I feel like Daddy Five," J said, "'cause I'm the one who organizes everyone."

Road Roommates

There's no escaping each other on the road either. When they're traveling, the guys are still together. In fact, early on, they shared rooms. Abs and Scott usually shared a room while J, Ritchie, and Sean alternated rooming with each other or staying alone. "We used to share rooms when we first got together," Scott told *Superteen* magazine. "But, now we all have our own rooms. We like our privacy, so we just chill out on our own."

One way or another though, Scott says, they always wind up together. "We normally go and have meals together and if Abs has his

Nintendo, we'll end up hanging out in his room or we'll go into Ritchie's room and watch a film on pay TV or we order food."

It's The Things They Do

During downtime, Five tends to split into two groups, with Abs, Scott, and Ritchie going one way, and Sean and J the other. It's not that they don't all get along, it's just that they find they have a bit more in common. For one thing Abs, Scott, and Ritchie are all the same age—19. "It's difficult," Scott explained in *Smash Hits* magazine. "I mean, we all get on in the group, but me, Abs, and Ritchie spend a lot of time together, and J and Sean spend a lot of time together. A lot of people have picked up on that and are saying, 'Oh, that must be 'cause Five don't get on,' but it's not that. Collectively, as a group, we always come together when it's right—do you know what I mean?"

Depending on their moods, each Five guy is sometimes drawn to a different band member. It's all about male bonding, stress levels, and attitudes. "It depends how I'm feeling," Abs tried to explain in *Live & Kicking* magazine. "I could hate Sean one day and then be best mates with him the next. I can walk into a room and feel who's giving out the good vibes, and today that was Sean."

More than anything else, what the five lads have found binds them together is that they're each a little odd in their own way. "We're a bit out there. I reckon we're all a bit mentally challenged," J joked with *Teen Beat* magazine. "Seriously, we're a strange bunch of guys. Any one of us on our own is enough, but then you get five of us together and . . . [shakes his head]."

"Wherever you come from there's always that one person who's really weird . . ." Scott began.

". . . The person who's a bit loud and sort of weird and absolutely over the top," J finished. "We're like five of him."

5

abs

"I am what you see and I don't pretend to be anything else," is how nineteen-year-old Abs described himself in *Live & Kicking* magazine. "I like to be taken seriously too."

Band mate Sean describes Abs a different way. "He's laid back but strong-headed. Sometimes he's completely silent and other times he won't stop talking."

Though he admits to having mood swings, Abs says, "I like my personality. Sometimes I'm really hyperactive, over the moon and happy, and sometimes I'm quite chilled out and quiet. I understand myself so much more since being in the band." Sounds like Abs has his feet firmly planted on the ground.

"I don't drink and I don't take any drugs. I've got too much common sense and high morals, big time. It's just the way I've been brought up," Abs added. Abs has fond memories of growing up and credits his dad for his musical inspiration and his mom for her support. To this day, they're still supportive. "They come see us play all the time," he told *All-Stars* magazine.

Baby Abs

On June 29, 1979, Kay and Turan Breen gave birth to their only child, Richard Abidin Breen in Enfield, England. Enfield's population is about 100,000 and it lies just north of London in Middlesex county. It was a fine setting for young Abs to grow up in.

Abs' childhood was far from ideal, however. His parents divorced when he was young and he was raised solely by his mother. Although, Abs' father did play an important role in his life. As a musician himself, he was an early influence on Abs. "My mom can sing, but she's never made anything of it. My dad's Turkish and I'm half Turkish and he's in a Turkish band," he told *Teen Beat* magazine. "He's got his own little group that would do weddings and all that kind of stuff."

The music rubbed off on Abs and he began singing earlier than he can remember. "I was about three, I think," he said in *Superteen* magazine. "Not professionally. I was just singing around. I was always around music." The inspiration for his career aspirations also came from someone a bit more famous. "For me, ever since I was young, it's always been Michael Jackson," Abs told *16* magazine. "From a really early age, I've, like, grown up on him. That was all I'd listen to when I was young, and also old school, jungle, that kind of stuff. That's why now I'm into deejaying."

Mama Abs

Mom supported Abs' love of music too. "I remember my first keyboard. It cost twenty pounds and that was a lot of money to a single mother," Abs recalled in *Smash Hits* magazine. "I had to wait a while to get it, but when I did, I cleaned it every day and kept it nice. I still have it to this day." Abs put his new instrument to good use, forming a band with his cousin. "Me and my cousin Izzy were trying to make a band when I was about eight," Abs told *Teen Beat* magazine. "I played the keyboard and we tried to write our own songs. I remember one. It was called 'Heartbreaker.'"

Abs did okay in school and took a particular liking to art and drama classes, but "I started hanging around with the wrong people and cutting school," Abs revealed in *Smash Hits* magazine. "I was picked on a few times at secondary school," Abs admitted in *Live & Kicking* magazine. "It wasn't for any particular reason. Since then I've learned to walk away from situations like that."

One thing Abs never had any trouble with was girls. "I've been told it so many times since I was little—'You're gonna be a real looker!'" Abs says. But, as gorgeous as he is, Abs hasn't the least bit of arrogance about his looks. "I get loads of letters from fans saying, 'You're really gorgeous,' but I don't see myself as anything special. I just hope that they're right," Abs confessed to *Live & Kicking* magazine. "But, I don't look into the mirror thinking, 'Yeah, you're a good-looking chap!' I'm not like that."

Abs is the same way about seeing himself on TV. "I don't like watching myself. I like performing, but I don't like watching myself," Abs revealed in *Bop* magazine. "All the others can say, 'Abs, you look really good,' but, I'm like, 'No, I look really stupid.' " Want to know why Abs wears hats so often? It's because "every day is a bad hair day," he told *Teen Beat* magazine. "I have mad hair as soon as I wake up in the morning."

Handling Success

Abs says the proudest achievement of his life was being accepted into the respected Italia Conti Performing Arts College. A degree would have to wait however, because Five came calling. Since then, Abs' life has changed quite a bit. "It's fun, you enjoy it," he explained to *Teen Beat* magazine. "It's hard work, but it's not like work. I look forward to doing it in the future still."

He's still getting used to all the attention too. "I'm so much more aware of photographers and fans being around. I don't reckon I'll ever get used to that," Abs told *Live & Kicking* magazine.

When Abs has extended time off he heads home. "I try, every opportunity I get, to go home and see my family," he told *Superteen* magazine. Unfortunately, those long breaks are few and far between. Abs' parents make the breaks seem shorter by coming to see him and his band mates perform every chance they get. "It's nice when your family comes to see you," Abs told *All-Stars* magazine. "When you're performing, you're trying to spot them out in the crowd, and when you do, it's like, aaaahhh!"

"It's really difficult," Abs explained. "We miss so much of our family and friends. We can be away for four months at a time. That's the worst part of all." As for the best part? "The best part is performing, traveling the world, making videos. Just getting out there on the stage with a mike and all these fans," he concluded.

Take Five

He may be an upright moral guy, but Abs is quick to remind, "I do take risks though." Like bungee jumping, for instance. "It was wicked," Abs told *Live & Kicking* magazine. "I've also heard about this thing where you jump out of a plane into a net that's suspended between two other planes below. I'd love to do that!" Easy Abs, don't you worry about getting hurt or dying even? "Nah, but I do worry about the people I'm leaving behind. Someone once read my tea leaves and told me that I'm going to die young. It doesn't bother me. I'm just going to enjoy myself while I can."

A few of the safer ways in which Abs enjoys himself include seeing movies, going online, and deejaying. He likes to spin records at home too. "I'm into anything with a big bass sound," he says and his CD collection has gotten out of control. "The record company gets us CDs and I've got loads," he told *Tiger Beat* magazine. "R & B, soul, dance music, everything—it's eclectic."

"I love my laptop. I'm always on my computer," he told *Superteen* magazine. When he's not on his Sony PlayStation, that is. "I'm a bit of a games-aholic," he says. Abs also likes to go shopping. He spends most of his money on PlayStation games, CDs, and clothes. "My favorite type of clothing is casual, everyday stuff," he says. But his next purchase will be a bit more expensive. You see, Abs recently got his driver's license and, as soon as he has the time, he plans on buying himself a new car.

His Lady Friend

This may come as a shock, so sit down before you read this section. Abs has a steady girlfriend. She's a pretty, young actress from London named Danielle. She's one of the stars of the off-beat, but true-to-life British comedy *EastEnders*. They've been dating for over two years and Abs isn't at all hesitant to admit he is head over heels for her.

To give you an idea of what Danielle means

to Abs, he has a stuffed animal zebra named Zebby that he hugs when he misses her. Danielle was given the cuddly toy when she was two and she gave it to Abs as a reminder of her love. Zebby now lives atop the cupboard in Abs' house.

"How do I know I'm in love? I dunno," Abs pondered in *Live & Kicking* magazine. "Danielle is the first and last thought of the day. She's just always on my mind." He also says, "Women are great, but they cost you loads." This might have something to do with his phone bill. Because he and Danielle are apart so much, he jokes that his average monthly phone charge approaches "One hundred million pounds!"

Being apart for long stretches is difficult for any relationship, but Abs says their situation is unique. "She's an actress, so it works out the same way," he explained in *Teen Beat* magazine. "She's on a British TV show, so she understands my being away all the time. She's away a lot too. It's hard, but I think at the end of the day, everyone needs someone to love."

Just The Facts

Full Name: Richard Abidin Breen
Nickname: Abs
Birth Date: June 29, 1979
Zodiac Sign: Cancer
Birthplace: Enfield, Middlesex, England
Height: 5 feet 9 inches
Eye Color: Brown
Hair Color: Black
Parents: Kay and Turan (divorced)
Siblings: None
Faves:
　　Singers/Groups: R. Kelly; Brian
　　　McKnight
　　Book: No particular title
　　Food: Mom's shepherd's pie
　　Place: EuroDisney
　　Sport: Soccer
　　Spice Girl: Ginger
Hobbies: Going to movies; deejaying; surfing
　　the Net; Sony PlayStation
Worst habit: Mood swings

Dislikes: Smoking, drugs, drinking, and fake
  people
Most like to meet: No one in particular
Most embarrassing moment: "My mum
  pulled down my trousers and smacked my
  bum in front of my friends. I was about
  eight at the time."

Tasty Tidbits

- Abs is half Irish and half Turkish.

- Abs speaks Turkish (he learned from his dad)
  and he also speaks some German (he learned
  in school) but says he's forgotten quite a bit.

- His mom wanted to name the group
  "Golden Studs."

- After seeing J skydive, Abs wants to give it a
  try too.

- Abs plays the piano and keyboards . . . but
  he ain't much of a cook. "I'm not too good in
  the kitchen," he says.

- He can't stand anchovies. "I flippin' hate 'em, man!" he told *Smash Hits* magazine. "They make me gag. They're so disgusting, I'm always pickin' 'em off stuff."

6
j

Although twenty-two-year-old J Brown is the oldest and most outspoken member of Five, he is by no means the band leader. "He's the daddy of the group," Abs told *Tiger Beat* magazine. "He makes sure we get up in the morning and we're where we should be, but he's not the boss. Oh, no."

J is tough. He's a muscular guy with a buzz cut and a big tattoo, and he doesn't smile much. He also comes on strong, often leading with his mouth. "J is a loudmouth, says what he likes, likes what he says," Scott explained in an interview with *Superstars* magazine. "He's really a nice lad though. A lot of people get him wrong. A lot of people think he's horrible, and he's loud and he's rude. He just speaks his mind."

In truth, there is a lot more to J than what you see. He is smart, responsible, funny, a good friend to his band mates, and knows how to have a good time. He is also dead serious about his music. "People often get the wrong opinion about me," J told *Live & Kicking* magazine. "They think I'm stand-offish, but I'm just a straightforward, down-to-earth, nice, normal guy."

Sweet Baby J

Jason Paul Brown was born June 13, 1976, in Aldershot, a small town in southern England not far from London. Baby J was brought home where he would be raised, with his older sister Donna, by his parents, Justin and Marilyn. His earliest memory is of "tipping a bowl of spaghetti over my head 'cause I didn't want to eat." J moved around a bit since his father was in the military. It may seem to be a confusing and turbulent way to grow up, but, in reality, all the relocating and traveling helped shape J into the well-rounded, open-minded, and mature guy he is today.

J's parents were also largely responsible for

the care and feeding of this pop star in the making. When asked by a reporter who his childhood hero was, he said, "My parents." J learned to be forthright, honest, and sure of himself from his father. He learned about tenderness from his mom. "I'm very close to her," he says. J was loved, supported, and taught right from wrong. That he turned out to be such a wild lad must have to do with something else. "I remember nearly falling off the third floor balcony of our flat in Germany when I was six. My sister pulled me back inside in the nick of time," he told *Live & Kicking* magazine.

From when J was knee high to his mom, he began to love music. He'd listen to it, dance to it, and sing along with it. Though Mama J and Papa J were supportive of his musical interests, they were quite surprised to find their son had a nice singing voice. "My mom can't sing a note at all and both my parents are tone deaf," J told *Tiger Beat* magazine. "I used to wonder if I was the milkman's son! Then I found out my grandma used to sing."

J kept up with the singing, and by listening

to music with his parents, sister, and friends, he developed a liking of all sorts of different sounds. "I listen to all different forms of music. I have all different types in my CD collection— some soul, '80s, stuff like that," he told *Superteen* magazine.

J went to school where he took classes, played sports, and made loads of friends. He was always smart but was a bit of an under-achiever. "I could've walked out of school with all A grades, but I messed around all the time," he admitted in a *Live & Kicking* interview. "I always saw myself as being on the same level as the teachers, so if they said anything which I thought was stupid, I'd tell them." Where did all this rebellion come from? "I've had a bad temper since being a kid and I've always had a problem with being bossed around," he continued. "Even when our manager tells us to be ready NOW, I'll be like, 'No, I'm still getting my stuff ready.'"

Fortunately, J was never so disagreeable with his peers. "I'd never bully anyone else. I despise bullies," he said. "I might have a laugh at people if they're wearing funny clothes, but I'd never laugh at someone if they had something physically wrong with them."

The J Bird Flies

In high school, J learned the meaning of responsibility. In addition to helping out around the house, he took on several jobs, one working in a warehouse and another doing magazine sales. He learned more about himself as a teen and figured out that music was his true calling. "For me, it's like something that's always been inside me. Since as far back as I can remember, I've wanted to do music," he explained in *All-Stars* magazine. "All through school, people would say, 'What are you going to do?' I always said, 'I know I'm going to do something with music.'"

Upon graduating from high school, J joined a hip-hop band called Prophets of Da Funk, who had a pretty good following. He rehearsed and performed local gigs with the group and set up recording equipment in his bedroom at home. "Before I got into Five, I was doing a

totally different thing," he told *Tiger Beat* magazine. "I would write some soul and stuff like
that." J helped out other local bands as well as
his own, trying his hand at producing, song writing, mixing, and recording. He also enrolled in
college as a backup plan.

Through it all, J's parents remained behind
him. "My parents have backed me all the way,"
he told *16* magazine. "I mean, I'm twenty-two
years old now and I went to college and my parents supported me through that. It was as big, if
not bigger, dream come true for them as it was
for me." Then J went to an audition and met up
with his future band mates. Within a matter of
weeks, they signed a contract and were off to
Sweden to record an album. Suddenly, there
was no need for a backup plan.

Taking It All In

"It's cool. It's still coming as a bit of a surprise,"
J told *All-Stars* magazine about Five's success.
As is the case with his rocky personality, J has
learned that the music industry also has its ups

and downs. "The best part is the performing and the traveling and the working in studios. The worst part is definitely the lack of sleep and the lack of decent food."

J misses more than just a good meal though. "There is definitely a downside to doing what we do, especially if you've got a really close family," he told *Teen Machine* magazine. "We get so busy, it's hard to see everybody, especially our friends outside the band. When we do get a bit of free time, we all rush home to see our families, so, it's tough to make time for your mates too."

The sacrifices you must make is the price you pay for celebrity and J accepts that. "We could all be stuck at home," J told *Tiger Beat* magazine. "I could still be stuck at home near Manchester in England doing what I was doing before, which was not working, trying to get a record deal, producing other people's stuff. I was jealous of people who had record deals. Now, instead I'm going to New York and L.A., Belgium and all over. We see different cities, different cultures, different people."

Despite all of his ability and desire, J knows

he'd never be where he is today if not for his family. In the *Five* album notes, he wrote, "First and foremost I would like to thank the most important people—my dad, Justin, mom, Marilyn, and sister, Donna, for always being there and giving me the love and support that I needed while trying to achieve my dreams."

A Few Sandwiches Short Of A Picnic

"Some people think I'm a bit nuts," J told *TV Hits* magazine. This is partly because he's loud and in your face, but mostly because he's a daredevil. Like his partner in crime, Abs, J also likes to go bungee jumping, as well as cliff diving and parachute jumping. "I like doing stupid, dangerous things 'cause they give me a buzz," J told *Smash Hits* magazine. "Life's a bit boring otherwise, isn't it?"

Life's never boring when J is around. He has a raucous sense of humor and loves to play pranks on his band mates. He also has a bit of fun with himself. He has an eyebrow ring, a tattoo and, at one time, J had a beard long enough to touch his chest.

He also once fancied himself a body builder. For a while he followed a strict diet and lifted weights for two hours every day. J has found it impossible to keep up this regimen as part of a touring band, however. "We used to try to get exercise and watch what we ate before the band. We all want to do it, but if you're working until eleven at night and have to get up early in the morning, you want to get some sleep too," he told *All-Stars* magazine. "It takes a toll on your body when you're traveling so much and working so much. We just have to survive on junk food most of the time."

Some of the more normal things that J does in his spare time include lifting weights, hanging out with his band mates, and listening to music. He especially likes hip-hop. "We don't get much free time," J told *Teen Beat* magazine. "If we do get any, and we're home, we usually just veg out in front of the TV with the PlayStation or Nintendo 64 and play video games all night till the early hours of the morning."

Just The Facts

Full Name: Jason Paul Brown
Nickname: J
Birth Date: June 13, 1976
Zodiac Sign: Gemini
Birthplace: Aldershot, England
Height: 5 feet 10 inches
Eye Color: Blue
Hair Color: Brown
Parents: Marilyn and Justin
Siblings: Older sister, Donna
Faves:
    Singers/Groups: Tupac Shakur
    Movie: *Dawn of the Dead*
    Book: *Valley of the Lights*
    Food: Chinese
    Place: Canada and Sweden
    Drink: Orange Juice
    Sport: Soccer
    Spice Girl: "Absent Spice—I'm not a fan"
Hobbies: Weight lifting; listening to music;
    Sony PlayStation
Worst habit: Losing his temper

Dislikes: Taxis

Most like to meet: "I'd have loved to have met Tupac [Shakur]"

Most embarrassing moment: "Forgetting the lyrics to a song in front of three hundred people at a music competition which everyone said I was going to win—I came third."

Tasty Tidbits

- J is a man of distinguishing marks. He has an eyebrow ring, a tattoo on his right arm, and a scar on his right jawline.

- He remembers having an ugly bowl cut as a little boy.

- J roots for the Manchester United soccer team.

- When he was younger, he had a crush on Raquel Welch.

- J has a teddy bear that he keeps which his sister bought for him as a birthday gift.

7

ritchie

On the surface, it's simple to judge nineteen-year-old Ritchie. One look at him and some may say, oh, he's just a pretty boy. After all, he's got the look of a TV star, with twinkling blue eyes and a million dollar smile. He's also about as comely as they come, sporting pressed clothes that fit and match just so, and nary a hair out of place. But beneath Ritchie's gorgeous exterior lies a rather complex person, really. He's emotional and introspective and quite in touch with who he is and what he thinks. But despite the fact that he's all this, as well as a successful and famous recording artist, Ritchie is quick to remind us all that "I'm just one of the lads."

Even his band mates have trouble putting a finger on Ritchie. J tried to explain what he's like in *Superteen* magazine. "Rich is the more emotional one of the band, you can tell straight

away what he's thinking by looking at his face."
But J also added, "He's a hippie as well . . . a
modern day hippie."

You can't categorize Ritchie. He's soft-
natured, sensitive, and considerate, yet he's very
sure of what he has to say. Everything about
him, his looks, his posture, his manners, the way
he speaks, and even the way he walks is polished. It's almost as though he were raised in
royalty, until you delve deeper and realize that
this same lad was naughty as a child, and as a
teen he was the singer of a hard rock band. One
thing's for sure. Ritchie was meant to be a star.

Little Richard

On August 23, 1979, Peter and Kim Neville
gave birth to their third child, a fair-haired,
blue-eyed boy, who they would name Richard.
The delighted couple brought their new bundle
of joy back to their home in suburban
Birmingham. The family of five resided in
Solihul, a small town just on the outskirts of
Birmingham, England's second largest city after

London. Birmingham, a city of over a million residents, lies in Warwickshire county in central England.

Ritchie's earliest memory is of his parents splitting up. His dad left his mom when he was just two years old, but he remained a part of Ritchie's life. Otherwise, Ritchie had a fairly normal childhood. "I've been told I was a very cute and nice child, but I was quite loud," Ritchie told *Teen Beat* magazine. Just imagine how adorable he must have been as a toddler. "I came out of my mother's womb singing," he added.

Musical Mom & Pop

Indeed, music was a part of Ritchie's life from the day he was born. "I was always singing as a child," he recalled in *16* magazine. "There was a song that went, [sings] 'Hands up, baby, hands up,' and I used to sing that all the time when I was little." Such early influence came from his parents. "My mom and my dad are both singers and that's how they met," he explained in *All-*

Stars magazine. "They used to sing 'Bright Eyes' to me because I've always had really blue eyes and my dad would sing 'Rhinestone Cowboy.'"

Were Ritchie's parents pop stars too? Not quite. "My dad was very much a Neil Diamond/Tom Jones sort of thing with sideburns and all. I've seen pictures," he explained in *16* magazine. "My mom was more Barbra Streisand. In Britain there's two TV programs that are nationwide talent shows, *Opportunity Knocks* and *New Faces*. My dad went on one and my mom was on the other. There was a cassette of what she sang on it and I could not believe it! She could have been a major, major star. She's really attractive too."

Ritchie began following in their footsteps as soon as he was out of his crib. "I've been singing since I was a toddler. I went to school when I was four years old and I joined the choir," he told *Teen Beat* magazine. "I stopped doing the church choir after a while because I wanted to go out and play with my friends."

Rebel, Rebel

As a child, Ritchie was a bit of an imp. "I was quite bad, but I seemed to get away with things," Ritchie told *Smash Hits* magazine. "I can't tell you what, though. I don't think you could print them—it wouldn't set a very good example." He wasn't a fighter or a bad student or anything like that—Ritchie's a heart breaker, not a law breaker. But, as he aged, Ritchie had his share of growing pains and teen angst. "At thirteen, I was just becoming my own person," he told *Teen Beat* magazine. "I wasn't necessarily rebellious, but I was very much like, 'Don't tell me what to do,' but my mom, fortunately, understood and catered to that."

Ritchie and his mom didn't clash much, as she was busy running the pub she owns while he was busy with classes, his friends, and activities. Ritchie was difficult to figure as a teen too. On the one hand, he attended an exclusive private school in Birmingham, yet he also had a job working in a burger van and often pitched in at his mom's pub.

In school, Ritchie found plenty of outlets for his energies. "I did all the plays at school," he recalled in *Superteen* magazine. "I played Romeo in *Romeo and Juliet*. I was sort of known as the school actor." His acting prowess led to roles in the National Youth Theatre. He also played soccer and, of course, returned to music.

"I started singing in rock bands," he told *Tiger Beat* magazine. "We didn't have any serious ambitions and I knew it. It was just fun. I was in a band with my friends called Anal Beard." Ritchie is a big fan of alternative rock, especially Pearl Jam. As the lead singer of his garage band he'd emulate lead singer Eddie Vedder. He even went so far as to dress in "dingy, grungy clothes" and says he had trouble getting dates because of it. Now, as a snappily dressed, world famous pop star, he doesn't have such problems.

One Out Of Five Ain't Bad

Ritchie hadn't even finished high school when he auditioned for Five. Although he's very bright, he has no regrets about postponing a college education for his current music career. "I live a totally different life now," he explained in *Teen Beat* magazine. "Before, I was at school, singing in a band with my friends. Now, I'm traveling around the world, working every day."

That's not a bad trade-off, but certainly it must have been a difficult transition. "There's not a lot of time off and that's the downside," he added. "Contrary to popular belief, bands work very, very hard. You want to see your family more and enjoy your fame and money, but you really just don't have the time."

Ritchie has grown more used to his fame, warts and all. He can do without missing his family, gaining "fake friends," and not always having privacy, but he knows it all comes with the territory. "In some ways, sometimes I think I'd like to keep a real personal life," he revealed in *Teen Machine* magazine. "I like my freedom. But, I know if I have the chance to be that way, I will, but I can't help it. I've always wanted to do this and that's why I'm here."

It's hardly grinning and bearing it though, as Ritchie is excited about the success of his band.

"Obviously, we're over the moon," he expressed, as only he can, in *Teen Beat* magazine. "It's really picking up all over the world. We're becoming a global band and that's really cool."

Looking back on it all, Ritchie thanks his Mom first and foremost. In the *Five* album liner notes, he says, "Firstly, Mom, thanks for being there for me and making the sacrifices. I'll never forget it. . . . Thank you for the support, confidence and caring for me and for getting me closer to my dreams."

Surrey About That

Moving into the Five house in Surrey with his band mates was a bit of an adjustment for Ritchie, who was raised in an affluent household. Ritchie's mates don't call him Posh because he looks anything like Victoria Adams of the Spice Girls. He earned that nickname because he is refined and mild-mannered. But as Ritchie explained to *Smash Hits* magazine, the crudeness of some of his band mates is beginning to rub off on him. "Scott can have bad table manners, like when we go out somewhere nice. And Abs gets in moods where he takes a glass of water, sticks ketchup in it, then salt and pepper, then empties the ashtray into it, sticks in a flower and mixes it all around."

When he's not entirely disgusted by his band mates, Ritchie enjoys hanging out with them. "We all have a PlayStation and also like to go out," he says, but adds that he also enjoys spending time with his mates from back home too. To relax, Ritchie also spends a bit of time alone, reading, talking to family and friends on the phone, or rooting for his favorite soccer team (Aston Villa) on television. He also enjoys films, dance clubs, and loves the beach, especially when he's on vacation.

Just The Facts

Full Name: Richard Neville
Nicknames: Ritchie, Posh
Birth Date: August 23, 1979
Zodiac Sign: Leo
Birthplace: Birmingham, Warwickshire, England

Height: 5 feet 9 inches
Eye Color: Blue
Hair Color: Blond
Parents: Kim and Peter (divorced)
Siblings: Older sister Tracy, older brother Dave
Faves:
  Singer/Group: Pearl Jam
  Actor: Sean Connery
  Book: *The Adventures of Adrian Mole*
  Food: Chinese
  Drink: Tea (two sugars)
  Place: Cape Town, South Africa
  Sports: Rugby, soccer
  Spice Girl: Baby
Hobbies: Going to dance clubs; listening to
  music
Worst habit: Biting his nails
Dislikes: "Big-headed, arrogant people"
Most like to meet: Eddie Vedder of Pearl Jam
Most embarrassing moment: "We were
  waiting for our luggage in Schiphol Airport
  in Amsterdam and had been spotted by
  some fans. We were chatting and signing

pictures when I saw some boxer shorts that looked like mine traveling loose around the luggage conveyor. I then realized that my bag had burst open and they were mine! To make matters worse this excited the girls who grabbed them and ran off. The problem is, I can't remember if they were clean or not. I hope they were!"

Tasty Tidbits

- Ritchie treasures his jewelry because it was all bought for him by his family. The ring he wears was a sixteenth birthday gift from his mom and it bears a personal inscription.

- His favorite song of all time is "Jeremy" by Pearl Jam.

- Ritchie has had a recurring nightmare that he's falling off a castle. "Every time I go to a castle now, I get a funny feeling."

- "I'm told I look like both my mom and dad. I've got a lot of both."

8

scott

It's been said that the British have an offbeat sense of humor (think *Austin Powers, Monty Python,* etc.). It's also a common perception that rockers are often wild and a bit out there (if not entirely bizarre like Busta Rhymes or Marilyn Manson). Meanwhile, teenage boys are said to be wildly energetic, girl crazy, and immature. So, what do you call someone who fits into all three of these categories? Completely bonkers or Scott Robinson.

To say that nineteen-year-old Scott is a horse of a different color would be an understatement. He sports strange haircuts, follows a diet that no one can make sense of, and has a rather peculiar sleeping pattern. When he does get his winks in, watch out. "Scott's just nonstop, battery charged," Abs spilled in *Tiger Beat* magazine. "At five o'clock in the morning he'll be singing Boyz II Men out the window."

"At half past three on the dot every day, he goes completely mental," J adds.

Scott can be dead serious at times too, like when it's time for the band to go on stage or into the studio. But, rest assured, when the work is done, Scott's the first one with a lampshade on his head. "People say I make them laugh and I talk quite a lot too," Scott told *Teen Beat* magazine.

Never make light of the group joker. Every good band has one guy who eases the tense moments on the road with a well-timed joke. The Backstreet Boys have Brian Littrell, 'N Sync has Chris Kirkpatrick and even Hanson has crazy little Zac. Five has Scott Robinson, and he can outwit all the others combined.

A Clown Is Born

On November 22, 1979, Scott James Tim Robinson was born in Basildon, Essex, England. Basildon is a small town of about 50,000 people in the south of Essex county, which lies in southeast England. After World War II, Basildon was designated a model residential community, which is sort of ironic when you realize that Five's self-proclaimed "nutter" (Brit speak for crazy person) was sprung from there.

Scott's parents, Mick and Sue, sent him and his two sisters to public school in Essex. Scott's had boundless energy since he was first born. "I was the loudmouth, the class clown and always in trouble at school," he told *Superteen* magazine. "I never did any work and was always jumping on tables and such. I think I must have liked detention."

Scott continued to sniff out trouble as he matured too. *Live & Kicking* magazine asked him what he was like as a teen. "Pretty much the same as now—cheeky, mouthy. I hung around with the wrong people for a while and got into a bit of police trouble. Nothing drastic, just coppers stopping us in the street. Being a big mouth, I always answered them back."

Fortunately, Scott found more constructive uses for his rather spirited behavior. He began playing basketball and acting in school plays. Scott really found his calling with acting and discovered he thrived on the attention. As a teen he attended the prestigious Sylvia Young Stage School. Singer Billie Piper was one of his class mates and Emma "Baby Spice" Bunton had graduated just a few years before him. Through the school, Scott landed work in television commercials, but when he heard about an audition for a certain pop band, he put his acting career on hold.

Parental Guidance Is Suggested

From when he was just a tot, Scott's whole family inspired him. His two sisters sang to him and his mom took him to his first concert, John Denver. Now, Mr. and Mrs. Robinson are so proud of their accomplished son, they could bust. "It's like they are so happy for me," Scott said in *Tiger Beat* magazine. "My mom has, from day one, from the very first article in the first British magazine or newspaper, she rips it out. She can't stop now. She's spent hundreds of pounds on that and she has a scrapbook. I swear, it's, like, huge!"

Scott's family has been so supportive of his career that it's almost embarrassing. "Scott's mom and dad have seen every performance," J told *Superstars* magazine. "They've bought every magazine and every newspaper. I think Scott's dad is taking on an extra two jobs now from buying all the magazines."

Scott showed his gratitude in the *Five* album liner notes. "Firstly, I would like to thank my mom and dad for liking each other enough to let me be here. Without them, nothing's possible." He also thanked them with his generosity. "I haven't really bought much for myself. I spend money on my family," Scott confessed in *16* magazine. "I bought my dad a Toyota Previa. It's like a mini-van." He did buy himself two expensive toys however, a mini disc player and a digital video recorder.

Great Scott!

Scott couldn't be more ecstatic about his group's success. "We're very happy and my mom's proud," he gushed to *Teen Beat* magazine. He summed up the whole experience this way: "The best part is performing and the hardest part is getting up in the morning and not seeing your family."

Scott's not at all hesitant to admit he gets homesick. "I'm the one who's always nagging and moaning about 'Why do we have to be here? Why can't we be back home?'" he told *Superstars* magazine. "I really miss my bearings, where I come from. I've got a lot of friends. It's nice to go home and see them."

Maintaining ties is not so easy when you're constantly traveling. Scott has learned this difficult lesson. "When I joined the band, I had a lot more friends than I have now. I've only got a few true friends now, only like a handful—girls included," he added. "Now when I go home, people see me walking with one of my sisters and they'll yell, 'That's his girlfriend!' Then I get people calling her names and it really annoys me."

It drives Scott mad that a lot of people don't look at him the same way since he became famous. He insists he's the same person he always was. "When I go home, I find that people have been slagging me off. This one guy went, 'Scott thinks he's a right pop star. He hasn't spoken to us for ages,'" he recalled in *Live & Kicking* magazine. "I try and straighten them out. I went up to one guy and said, 'Look, mate, my hair might be a bit drastic, but I'm still the same lad.'"

A touring band's schedule can be grueling at times, as Scott has learned. "It's a lot of work," he told *Teen Machine* magazine. "You just get used to it. We've been doing it for quite a while now. The routines are hard, but we pretty much are used to it now."

Restless Sleeper

Scott's a late sleeper, which is odd considering he's usually one of the first to hit the hay. In fact, he and Abs usually share a hotel room on the road because they're the ones who usually go to bed the earliest. "If I don't sleep when I'm tired, I'll get really moody," Scott explained to *Teen Beat* magazine.

"He sits or sleeps all the time," J added, "and we're like, 'Scott, we're in New York or we're in Belgium. Let's go do something!' and he'll just go, 'Aw, I'm tired.' He's lethargic and then he gets these spurts like a little kid who's had too many Smarties." There must be some reason why a young, healthy chap would be so sluggish all the time. J suspects he has the answer. "The thing is, Scott has a strange diet," J continued. "This is a run down of what he eats, no exaggeration. He has fast food, junk food, pizza, beans, bread, milk, and mashed potatoes. That's all he eats, so he's never got any energy."

Finicky Eater

"I've been taking some vitamins," Scott told *Superteen* magazine. "Basically, I'm still a really bad eater. The other lads have gotten better, but I hardly eat anything. I still eat burgers. I'm very fussy."

"He's too particular. He goes into a restaurant and can't eat the sauces or the toppings," J tattled in *All-Stars* magazine. "He'll go into

McDonald's even and say, 'Can I have three plain burgers please?'"

"No, no, no," Scott chimed in. "It's three plain burgers, a large fries, a chocolate milk shake and eight tomato ketchups." If that sounds strange, wait until you get a load of the eating ritual Scott has.

"He lines up all the fries on each burger and then puts salt and ketchup on it," J begins. "Then he eats this thing like it's the best steak he's ever tasted. It could be the third time he's had McDonald's that day and he has a look on his face like it's a life-changing experience."

Hellish Haircuts

While he may be best known for his trademark spikes, Scott's had a number of bizarre hair styles over the years. He was once given the nickname Curtains, because "I had long floppy hair with a parting in the middle." But the worst haircut of all, Scott says, was when he was just a kid. "I had a curly perm when I was in *Peter Pan*," he told *Teen Beat* magazine.

"I take good care of my hair 'cause I quite like the way it looks," Scott said, but added, "I don't think I'm anything special though. I've got spikey hair and blue eyes. That's the only reason girls go, 'Ooooh!'"

Creating those porcupinelike quills atop his head is no small chore. To make his hair stand on end, as such, Scott must twist each individual spike with a dab of pommade. For photo shoots, he spends much more time than any of the other Five guys tending to his tresses. "It takes me about half an hour from scratch and when I sleep at night I don't brush it out. I just re-do it at the sides in the morning," he explained in *Live & Kicking* magazine. Scott recently gave up on his high maintenance spikes and has instead opted for a simple short hairdo. Stay tuned, however.

Aside from his odd relationship with his hair, Scott doesn't have a vain bone in his body. "For the past month, I've been looking in the mirror thinking, 'Oh my God! You ugly git!' We've been working so hard, I've had bags under my eyes and strange rashes," Scott confessed in an interview with *Live & Kicking* magazine.

Just The Facts

Full Name: Scott James Tim Robinson
Nickname: Spider
Birth Date: November 22, 1979
Zodiac Sign: Scorpio
Birthplace: Basildon, Essex, England
Height: 5 feet 11 inches
Eye Color: Blue
Hair Color: Brown
Parents: Sue and Mick
Siblings: Sisters Hayley and Nicola
Faves:
    Singer/Group: No Doubt
    Movie: *White Men Can't Jump*
    Book: *The Hobbit*
    Food: Pizza
    Drink: Cherry Coke
    Place: Florida
    Sport: Basketball
    Spice Girl: Scary
Hobbies: Listening to music; skating; Sony
    PlayStation

Worst habit: Eating junk food
Dislikes: "Most food"
Most like to meet: Michael Jordan
Most embarrassing moment: "Any time my hair isn't up to scratch."

Tasty Tidbits

- The other band members sometimes call him Spider because he's got such skinny legs.

- Scott once met Michael Jackson while on an audition.

- Five was on the *Smash Hits* Tour when Scott turned eighteen, so he got to celebrate in style. Joining in the rousing good time were other young pop stars like Peter Andre, All Saints, and N-Tyce.

- Scott says his childhood hero was Michael Knight from *Rider*.

- He once had a job selling bikinis in a market.

- Like Ritchie, Scott's a soccer fan, only he roots for Arsenal.

- Scott likes children so much he often volunteers to baby-sit. He looks forward to being a dad himself. "I love kids!" he enthused in *Live & Kicking* magazine. "I wanna wait until I'm twenty-two, but I've chosen their names already. I'll have a boy, Jordan, and two girls called Courtney and Remy."

9

sean

Seventeen-year-old Sean is a tough nut to crack. He doesn't talk much and appears to put up a tough front. It's a barbed wire fence of a façade and he only opens the gate for his family, closest friends, and band mates. Other Five guys say he's shy and cautious around those he doesn't know. Behind the façade, there's actually quite a bit to this young lad. He says he is "one of the serious ones in the band" and describes himself as "shy and emotional" while Ritchie says, "He's definitely not soppy, although he has a soft side too."

Sean is many other things, but, since one of them is reticent, we'll have to let his band mates do the talking. "Out of all of us, we thought Sean was going to be really normal because he was really quiet and everything," Scott explained in *Teen Beat* magazine, "and then we got to know him and he fits right in." In other words, like his fellow Fivesters, he's a bit eccentric.

"J says that I'm lazy," Sean added.

"People always meet us and say, 'Oh, Sean's the laid-back one of the group,' but it's really just that he's too lazy," J told *Superstars* magazine. "He's always like [*in a slow drawl*] 'Hi, I'm Sean.' He's not into what he's doing. He's the laziest." Sean's quite a messy roommate as well.

He's also stubborn. "He has strong opinions," Ritchie added, "and there's no changing his mind."

Lastly, Sean is wise beyond his years, which, according to J, has its good and bad points. "Really, he's got so much common sense. He's very old for his age. He's like a seventy-year-old man in a seventeen year old's body," J told *Tiger Beat* magazine. As for the downside, "He doesn't like modern technology," J said. "He can't work things like mobile phones. If Sean needs to make a call, I give him mine to use and he's like, 'What do I do?'" But all of these little peculiarities are just part of Sean's charm.

Sweet Li'l Sean

Sean Kieran Conlon was born May 20, 1981, in Horsworth, a nearby suburb of Leeds, in northern England. Leeds is a mid-size city in central Yorkshire county populated by about a half million residents.

From the first time baby Sean opened his mouth, he seemed destined to be a singer. He was born into a musical family and began singing when he was just four years old. "My dad sings and plays drums, my sister plays guitar, and my brother plays drums and deejays," he told *TV Hits* magazine.

Sean attended public school in Leeds, where he continued singing, played rugby, made friends, and got into a bit of trouble. "I wasn't terrible, but I was quite bad," Sean admitted in *Smash Hits* magazine. "I got distracted easily and wasn't interested in anything academic. I got bored and fell asleep in class all the time, never did my homework and generally enjoyed getting into trouble."

However, Sean's schooling was not a total

loss. He got a basic education, studied, and practiced music. He also developed into an outstanding rugby player, good enough to play on league teams, but he gave it up when he realized, "You can't do music with a smashed up face and no teeth."

The Child Prodigy

Sean began taking music seriously at a very early age and his parents were his greatest source of encouragement. Sean adopted the musical tastes of his parents and older siblings. To this day, he still listens to old school R & B like the Isley Brothers and Marvin Gaye as much as he does to modern artists like R. Kelly, Seal, and Jamiroquai. "I mostly listen to soul music— Marvin Gaye and the Jackson Five," he told *All-Stars* magazine.

Sean modeled his own singing style on those of his idols, and with voice lessons and lots of practice and guidance he began to show signs of developing the priceless pipes he has today. In time, Sean and his parents began to realize that he was born with a gift rarer than diamonds—a tender singing voice as smooth as silk. Such vocal ability cannot be taught, but it can be honed. Sean wrote his first song at nine, and with the help of his folks, he recorded his first demo when he was just eleven.

Not many young kids are so driven. Sean was different, as he explained in an interview with *Teen Beat* magazine. "I always used to say at school, 'When I'm famous and when I do this,' and people would say, 'You shouldn't say that because there are billions of people worldwide trying to do it.' I knew the desire was in me so strong, I actually couldn't picture myself doing anything else."

At thirteen, Sean was entered in Great Britain's Yamaha Young Pop Musician Singing Competition, a renowned talent showcase. Hopefuls from all over the country competed for the esteemed judges, Elton John and Andrew Lloyd Webber. Sean proudly took home the Young Composer of the Year award, which now remains on a shelf in his parents' home.

Sean was merely fifteen when he auditioned for Five, and was still in school when the band signed its recording contract. A tutor was hired to continue his lesson plans while he's in the band, but with Five's fast rising success, Sean has fallen behind in his studies. However, he does hope to graduate some day. It would make his mom and dad proud.

In the *Five* album notes, Sean thanked his folks. "I'd like to say thank you to Mom and Dad for supporting me all the way through thick and thin, and to the rest of my family for their support."

Still Just A Boy

Sean told *Teen Beat* magazine that "The hardest part [of being in a band] is the lack of sleep and food." But, it's well worth the sacrifice because "The best parts are traveling, recording, and performing." Beyond that, Sean is still getting used to the spotlight. "I think it's still a shock," he says.

All the attention from fans and media makes

him a bit nervous, and since he's a bit shy to begin with, this makes him a tough person to get to know. When he's onstage or with his band mates, he loses his inhibitions and is practically a different person. Because Sean is the youngest Five guy, he's an obvious target for his band mates to tease. Scott, Ritchie, Abs, and J taunt him about being the youngest, the laziest, and the shiest of the bunch. But Sean can give it right back, calling J grandpa and ribbing the other guys about their haircuts.

Sean still gets a big kick out of seeing himself and his band mates on TV. He finds the whole concept of watching himself to be weird, as he tried to explain in *Bop* magazine. "It's like, you know when your mom films you on a camcorder, and then she puts it on and plays it back? It's kind of like that." Sean's uneasy about posing for photo shoots as well. He seems to think he isn't very photogenic. "I feel like there's always something wrong with me," he said. "I look a bit uglier or something." Sean, baby, there are thousands of willing girls who strongly disagree with you.

J's His Boy

Sean's best friend in Five is J, although their relationship is more of a big bro/little bro situation. J and Sean look to one another for support since they don't get to see their parents as often as the other Five guys. "Mine and J's come the least to our shows," Sean lamented in *Teen Beat* magazine. "Mine can't so much because we live all the way down south."

Sean looks up to J, and, in turn, J looks after Sean. When Sean oversleeps, J wakes him up by jumping up and down on his bed. And if Sean's running late, or hasn't packed enough clothes for a trip, J's there to set him straight. "I do his washing and ironing and everything for him," J told *16* magazine. "He'll know we need like six or seven changes of clothes for a photo shoot and he'll turn up with, like, one creased T-shirt extra, along with whatever he's got on. We have to make him shave as well. He turns up for photo shoots, even for, like, the front cover of *Smash Hits* magazine, with, like, a shadow on his face."

J even provides guidance for Sean, as if he really is his little brother. "I play the instants (scratch off games) and I got a bit addicted at one time," Sean admitted to *Smash Hits* magazine. "I was buying them at every petrol station and J had to wean me off of them."

Sean even spent his vacation time with J in the Greek Islands. "We just had a really relaxing time," he told *Smash Hits* magazine. "Did we meet any girls? No, we didn't go there for that. We went there to chill out, not to party and go out all night."

In his free time Sean goes home to see his family and friends. Apart from that, he sleeps, listens to music, watches a bit of soccer on television, and plays Sony PlayStation. He lists his five favorite things in order as: "(1) writing music, (2) listening to music, (3) girls, (4) being in the band, and (5) sleeping."

Just The Facts

Full Name: Sean Kieran Conlon
Nickname: Gungi

Birth Date: May 20, 1981
Zodiac Sign: Taurus
Birthplace: Leeds, Yorkshire, England
Height: 5 feet 9 inches
Eye Color: Brown
Hair Color: Black
Parents: Kate and Dennis (divorced)
Siblings: Two sisters and two brothers
Faves:
 Singers/Groups: Marvin Gaye; the Isley
  Brothers; R. Kelly; Seal
 Actor: Eddie Murphy
 Book: *Kes*
 Food: Pasta
 Drink: Coke
 Place: Sweden
 Sport: Rugby
 Spice Girl: Scary
Hobbies: Listening to music; Sony PlayStation
Worst habit: Laziness
Dislikes: "People who think they're the best"
Most like to meet: R. Kelly
Most embarrassing moment: "Knocking
 over a table full of food at a party."

Tasty Tidbits

- Sean once tried to grow dred locks but "when I grew my hair out it went all fuzzy."

- His favorite snack is cheese and onion crisps.

- He plays keyboards and likes to write songs.

- Sean has had jobs doing removals and delivering newspapers.

- Sean's not a big fan of the Big Apple. "I found it really interesting, but I didn't like the way we were living there," he told *Smash Hits* magazine. "It's all too busy and desperate, I think."

10

coming to america

Though Five's record company in Europe is
RCA, Arista Records, their sister company
(both are owned by international music con-
glomerate BMG), handles the distribution and
promotion of their album in America. "We do
expect great things from Five," an Arista
Records executive said in *Faces in Pop* magazine. "We believe they are very special in their
approach and in their talent. We are very proud
of our association with them."

Conquering The States

By the time "When The Lights Go Out" was
released in North America, Five was already an
international sensation. So when the guys first
heard themselves on American radio and saw
themselves on American TV, it was another

accomplishment, but by no means a shocking one. "People know who we are now," Abs told *Bop* magazine. "So, it was a bit different, definitely."

"When The Lights Go Out" steadily climbed the Billboard Hot 100 Singles chart while it got steady radio play and was, at one point, the number one requested video on The Box. The single cracked the top ten and stayed there for most of the summer. It did even better at the record stores, where it sold over a half million copies en route to going gold. By the end of summer, Americans were humming the tune and knew all the words to "When The Lights Go Out." But, who were the cute guys in the video who sing it?

In September 1998, Five was to return to the United States for a full-fledged media blitz. Unfortunately, the exciting introductions would have to wait as Five got some very bad news. Denniz Pop, the most important producer of their debut album, who the guys spent several months working with, had died of cancer. Without a moment's consideration, Five postponed all of their upcoming engagements and flew to Stockholm, Sweden. At the funeral, Five mourned the loss of their mentor, co-worker, and friend with dozens of other musicians and record industry insiders. Pop had produced and co-written half of Five's songs, as well as shown J, Abs, Sean, Ritchie, and Scott their way around the studio. The loss was devastating, but the guys had little time to reflect.

Coast To Coast

From Sweden, Five flew to New York City where they were photographed and interviewed by *Seventeen, Teen Beat, YM, Superteen, Teen People, Tiger Beat,* and *16*. They dropped by radio stations and got featured in stories by the *New York Post* ("Invasion of the Spice Boys!") and *USA Today* ("Let's Hear It For the Boys: Britain's Five"), America's top selling newspaper. At the end of their week in the Big Apple, Five made a very special appearance.

Abs, Ritchie, Scott, J, and Sean held an autograph signing and then did an outdoor performance at the Virgin MegaStore in Times Square. What's the big deal, you ask? Times Square is the busiest, loudest, and brightest part of New York City. Located in midtown Manhattan, the area is aglow with blinding neon signs and bustling with tourists. It is a major intersection, a central conduit for trains and buses, the heart of the theater district, and also where the ball drops on New Year's Eve. Thrown in the middle of this were five young, unassuming guys from Great Britain.

"We did Times Square yesterday and the fans went mad!" Abs enthused in *Teen Beat* magazine.

"Yeah, it was mad, you know," Ritchie added. "Some of the fans were crying, some were screaming. 'Oh, my God!' was the general gist. Some were pinching my bum."

"There were a lot of people there," Scott gushed to *Superteen* magazine. "It's kind of weird to be big over here. Obviously, we're known in Europe, but for people to know the name Five is weird because we haven't been here long."

When the excitement wore down, Five boarded a flight to the West Coast—next stop, Los Angeles. In the land of sun, sand, and celebrities, Five granted interviews with *Teen* magazine, *Bop*, and even *Entertainment Tonight*. Like they did in New York, Five ended their L.A. stay in style, with an in-store appearance at a Sam Goody record store at City Walk near Universal Studios. Security wasn't prepared for what ensued. Seven hundred fans showed up to see Five perform a few songs outside the record store. They screamed and waved teen magazines in the air. Afterward, many of them were climbing over the barricades and one another to get an autograph or a handshake.

"We've come over to the States and it's such a big place. We didn't really expect to get the kind of reception we got here. It's cool," J told a *Teen Beat* magazine reporter.

Five Up Close

After a quick trip back to Europe for a few promotions in Italy and a concert in Essex,

England, Five came back to America with their sights set on TV. For the entire month of October, Five bounced back and forth between New York, Los Angeles, and Chicago granting interviews to news programs and taping talk show segments. They were in everybody's living room, popping up on *The Ricki Lake Show*, *Live! with Regis & Kathie Lee*, *The Howie Mandel Show*, *Roseanne*, *Good Day NY*, *Montell Williams*, *The Jenny Jones Show*, and *MTV Live*. They also pitched in at Nickelodeon's annual Big Help, where they performed a live, outdoor version of "When The Lights Go Out" to a delighted crowd of kids.

Five closed out this American go 'round with a performance at *Seventeen* magazine's New Star Showcase in New York City. While Ace of Base also performed and several prominent actors and models were on hand, it was immediately evident that the sold out crowd was there to see Five. Ritchie, Abs, J, Scott, and Sean only performed five songs, but it was a scrumptious appetizer for the fans on hand who were anticipating a more satisfying full tour in the near future.

As club music blared, Five came out on stage one at a time—Abs . . . Scott . . . Sean . . . J . . . Rich! The crowd pushed toward the stage as the guys opened the show with a rousing rendition of "Slam Dunk (Da Funk)." The five guys danced, hopped, and popped in unison. While Sean sang and J and Abs rapped, Rich and Scott got the crowd fired up when they ran at each other, jumped and bounced off each other's chests in midair.

Five then sent the crowd into a tizzy with "When The Lights Go Out." Scott showed off his new short haircut, sans spikes, while J rapped, Sean crooned, and Rich smiled and waved to girls in the crowd. Meanwhile Abs played into the audience's fever, running around touching their hands. After a memorable presentation of "It's The Things You Do" (which Five announced would be its second U.S. single) and a tender Rich and Scott duet of "Until The Time Is Through," J came out and asked the crowd, "Is everybody in the house having a good time?!" The crowd's cheers were met with a rocking performance of "Everybody Get Up."

"We want to release 'Everybody Get Up' as the next single here," J told *Teen Beat* magazine. "We all think it's a good single for America. Every time we perform it, the crowd always goes mad."

Out With A Bang

"I like America, but everything is so different , so weird," J told *16* magazine. "I like it when I'm here, but, after a while, I start wanting to get back home, back to normality." Five headed back to Europe in November and after a few weeks of promotional appearances in Holland and Germany and a string of television appearances in England, Five headed for Milan for the MTV Europe Awards. Five was nominated for two awards, Best Breakthrough Act (along with All Saints, Aqua, Eagle Eye Cheery, and Natalie Imbruglia) and Best Pop Band (along with Aqua, Backstreet Boys, Boyzone, and Spice Girls).

The night was magical for Five, and millions of viewers got to share in the excitement. After getting the whole arena up on their feet with a magical performance of "Everybody Get Up" that included thirty-five backup dancers, Five graciously accepted the MTV Viewers' Select Award. The award, voted on by pop fans all over Europe, is given to the band of the favorite video, essentially crowning the group Europe's favorite band. It's a tremendous honor, which the Spice Girls took home in 1996, the Backstreet Boys in 1997, and Five in 1998.

While it's nearly impossible to top such an achievement, Five did their best by spending the rest of November making more TV appearances and promotional appearances and performing all over Great Britain. The guys performed on *Top of the Pops, The Big Breakfast, Mad For It, The Pepsi Chart Show*, and brought the house down with two shows in one night in London.

The first show, hosted by *Top of the Pops*, took place at London's Sound Republic in Leicester Square and featured special guests (and friends of Five) Kavana and Matthew Marsden. To prove they're not just a boy band,

Five played a second gig that night at an over-eighteen club in London's Astoria. While the screams weren't quite as loud, the audience seemed to enjoy themselves nonetheless.

A Tour Taste

Exactly one year after they were named Best New Tour Group of 1997, Five again participated in the *Smash Hits* tour, only a lot can change in a year. "We can't believe we're gonna be headlining three dates, especially as this time last year no one know who we were," Abs told *Smash Hits* magazine. "The *Smash Hits* tour is a major thing to us—it's one of the places we started out. Last year's tour was one of the best times of our life—J and Sean only got twelve hours' sleep during the whole thing!"

For the 1998 *Smash Hits* tour, Five was joined by 911, Billie, Steps, Kavana, Matthew Marsden, Ultra, and B*Witched. Five headlined three shows over three consecutive nights in Newcastle, Manchester, and Sheffield. After a week of shows in the United States, they came back to do one last *Smash Hits* show. Readers of *Smash Hits* magazine voted Five the Top Pop Band of 1998 in the Reader's Poll. This meant Five had the honor of also headlining the finale in London and hosting the Poll Winners Party.

With exactly no time to enjoy their newest achievement, Five was headed back to the United States again. They came back to give the United States a taste of Five alive before they would begin rehearsals in anticipation of a 1999 concert tour. Five played nine radio shows in twelve days all across the United States. The three days in between were reserved for flying back to London for the *Smash Hits* tour finale.

Starting with a WXYV show in Baltimore, Maryland, and a Z104 show in Washington, DC, Five headed to Memphis for their WKSL performance and then Dallas for the WHKS show before heading back to England. Upon returning, they headed for Minneapolis, Minnesota, where they packed the enormous parking lot outside the Mall of America, the largest shopping mall in the United States. Over the next four days they played radio shows in Albany,

New York, Flint, Michigan, and two in California—KZQZ in San Francisco and KDND in Sacramento. By the end, Americans were salivating for more, but they would have to wait as Five was to begin their 1999 concert tour in Europe.

Throughout all this excitement, "It's The Things You Do" continued its ascent up the American pop charts and "Until The Time Is Through" was released as the fifth single in Europe. Meanwhile, unbeknownst to American pop fans, they were about to get clobbered over the head with "Everybody Get Up." Would it be as big a hit in America as it was in Europe? Only the future will tell.

11

the future of five

Now that Five is so popular and has had so many hit songs, how about a full-blown, around the world concert tour? "We've been thinking about one now," J told *All-Stars* magazine. "We'll probably be doing a small theater tour of Britain over the first few months of 1999, and, depending on how that goes, take it into Europe and maybe the States. For the States, we really want to wait until we have an hour show together—it's not worth coming over to do three songs."

At the conclusion of their "tune up" tour of the United States, Five spent a few weeks in rehearsals, working with their choreographer on some new dance moves and performance routines. This is all in preparation of Five's 1999 tour, only that will likely begin a month later than J said because a few minor projects have popped up for the group.

First off, Five signed a year-long contract to promote Pepsi Cola in Great Britain. Similarly to the campaign the Spice Girls did in 1997, Five will record a new version of "Generation Next" for commercial use. Additionally, twelve-packs of Pepsi Cola will be sold with a CD single of their version included in the packaging. Each band member will reportedly be paid 500,000 pounds (about $750,000) to do Pepsi television and radio ads through 1999. That's a lot of Sony PlayStation games! With these earnings, plus earnings from their forthcoming tour and second album, you can bet the guys won't be sharing a house much longer.

The second thing that will be keeping Five busy at the start of 1999 is a Disney Channel special they'll be working on. In 1998, 'N Sync's *In Concert* special scored record ratings and drove the group's album sales through the roof. Five's special will be similar, with them touring the amusement park, doing interviews and performing, only their *In Concert* special will be taped in Disney Land in California, not Disney World in Florida, where 'N Sync's took place.

The Five Disney Channel special will air in the spring of 1999.

Following Up A Winner

Most likely, Five will begin work on a second album in the fall of 1999. While, for the most part, they will stick to the hip-hop pop formula that worked for them the first time around, there will certainly be some changes. For one thing, producer Denniz Pop, who played a massive role in the creation of their first record, is no longer with us. Because of that, and also because the group is now more experienced and confident, they plan on having even more of a hand in the creation of the songs on their follow-up CD.

"We make sure that we get to write on our albums," J explained to *Teen Beat* magazine. "Like, on our second album, we're not going to let anybody write all of our music. It is something that's important to us. We've all been doing this stuff beforehand, so it's something that we enjoy." What J means is that Five is going to at least co-write every single song on their next CD, not two out of three as was the case on *Five*. They may also completely write the lyrics and music for a few songs on their own.

Don't count out the possibility of Five getting creatively involved in the studio in other ways too. For one thing, Abs and Sean both play piano and keyboards and may want to sample their instrumental talents on a song or two. Also J has prior experience producing and Abs has done deejaying work. Perhaps they'll try their hands at producing, mixing, arranging, and recording as well. They learned quite a bit the first time around in Sweden and have been itching to get back in the studio after two years of touring, promotion, and making videos.

Promoting the next CD won't be nearly as exhausting for Five or for their record companies. This time around, everybody knows who Five is and what they are capable of—there's no need for an introduction. Music writers, radio stations, record stores, and especially pop fans don't need to be sold on their looks, character, and talents. The second Five CD will practically sell itself.

Dispelling Rumors

At the end of 1998, rumors were flying that J was leaving the band to pursue a solo career. After all, he is the oldest, the most outspoken, and also the one with the most experience, having been a producer and a member of another band before Five. However, this all started with the usual Internet chatter and a few quotes taken out of context. J set the record straight in an interview with *Smash Hits* magazine. "Basically, I came back off my holiday a week ago and got told by various people that I'd left the band, that the other guys hated me, and that I hated them. Apparently, I told them I couldn't be bothered any more." What a bunch of rubbish! J and his band mates were equally upset by the rumors, but have since learned to laugh off such nonsense. "I've got no idea where [the rumor] came from," J continued. "Obviously, it's not true, 'cause I'm here!"

Actually, J, like his band mates, has big plans for the future. "We all have things we want to do while we're in Five, as well as for after Five," J told *16* magazine.

Ritchie's goal is "obviously to make Five the biggest success possible," he told *Superteen* magazine. "Then, you know, we're also realistic. The Spice Girls are kind of fizzling out and seem to be going their separate ways. Take That didn't make it in America but they were massive everywhere else, and they split up. So, we know we won't last forever, and I'd like to build up a career, maybe act."

Abs said his goal is for Five "to be the biggest band in the world, probably what every other group wants." He said we can count on Five to stick around for a while. "As long as people want us around, we'll want to keep doing it."

For now, count on Five to stay together for quite a while, but a ways down the road, you can expect to see all five of them in different places. Abs will likely be producing, J sees himself starting his own record label, Ritchie talks of returning to acting, and Sean's silky smooth and soulful voice has solo artist written all over it. As for what Scott will be doing, that's anyone's guess. But, it's a safe bet that whatever he's up to, everyone around him will be laughing.

Message To The Fans

The *Five* album liner notes conclude with a collective message from the guys. "A huge Five thank you to all the radio stations, TV, press, and everyone who has believed and propelled us along our Five journey. Lastly, we pay a huge Five respect to the fans and fellow nutters out there who have made all this possible—the best is yet to come."

Five took the world by storm in 1998. They topped the charts in Europe, Asia, and Australia with a flurry of hit songs and got the word out in America that there was a new great pop act in town. In a very short while Five went from newcomers to in-demand international stars who are hot on the heels of the Backstreet Boys. With BSB holed up in the studio recording their follow-up record and Five about to launch a

world tour, there may be a changing of the pop
guard in 1999. By the summer of 1999, Five will
be the name on everybody's lips, much the way
BSB was in 1998 and the Spice Girls in 1997.
Make way for Abs, Scott, J, Ritchie, and Sean in
'99—it's Five's year!

12

boyfriend material?

If you had to choose just one guy from Five to be your boyfriend, who would it be? They're all super talented, gorgeous, and famous, so picking which one is kind of like deciding on a flavor of ice cream—you can't go wrong! Ritchie is a sweet, sensitive guy with the face of an angel, but Abs is sexy, charming, and romantic. J is adventurous and has muscles to spare, but Scott would put you in stitches and Sean can melt you with his warm smile or his velvety soft voice. It's practically impossible to choose, but you can't have 'em all! Here is a breakdown of the romantic side of each Five guy, just in case you ever have to decide which one will be your next boyfriend.

Abs

If you spend your nights dreaming of Abs, then reading about his girlfriend in chapter five must have really bummed you out. Well, before you lose any sleep over it, just remember, Abs isn't married and he's still just 19. That he's hopelessly devoted to his girl is very telling. "I'd do anything for the woman in my life," Abs revealed in *Bop* magazine. If that woman were you, he'd treat you like gold just the same.

"I'm a bit of a romantic," Abs says. He's not kidding either. When asked about his favorite romantic moment, he recalls a rainy evening stroll with his girl down a Paris street on Christmas. He's also quite sensitive. "Boys need a lot more love and tender care [than girls]," Abs told *Live & Kicking* magazine. "They put on this hard, 'Yo! I'm your man' image, but you can't get by in life without being loved."

Robert Smith of the legendary Brit band the Cure once said "Boys Don't Cry." Abs disagrees wholeheartedly. "*Titanic*—I bawled throughout the whole film," he revealed in *Live & Kicking* magazine. "Stress makes me cry too—when everything gets on top of me or I have problems at home. I'm not afraid of crying though. It helps relieve the pressure."

Abs has adored women since long before he met his girlfriend. In fact, he once took ballet lessons just to be the "only lad in a class full of girls in leotards." He didn't even scoff at the idea of adding a girl band member to Five when *Live & Kicking* magazine put the question to him. "It might be nice, but it could work out the wrong way. I could imagine Sean getting off with her and then her boyfriend starting on me!"

Type he goes for: Abs lists his ideal woman as "The woman I love." For the record, she's blond with green eyes and not too tall. Otherwise, Abs has said he likes girls who are feminine and dislikes girls who are "in love with themselves."

Celebrity crush: His girlfriend, Danielle. She's an actress.

Telling quote: Abs defines love as "thinking

of the person every minute of the day and wanting to be with them."

Abs is a Cancer, born June 29. Many astrologers consider Cancer to be the most romantic of all star signs. After all, Cancers are typically loving, sympathetic, protective, emotional, and loyal. How's that for a tasty boyfriend recipe? In addition, Cancers usually have terrific memories, so, it's not likely Abs would ever forget your birthday. On the down side, Cancers can be hyper-sensitive, letting the slightest thing upset them. They are also often too quick to criticize their loved ones. Cancers seek out a significant other who is tender and affectionate above all else.

J

In an interview with *Bop* magazine, J was asked which of the single guys in Five (everyone but Abs) has the most luck with girls. "I swear on my life, none of us! There's just nothing when it comes to females," he lamented. It's certainly not for lack of interest. J says, "I can sniff a beautiful woman at twenty paces."

The problem, believe it or not, is that J's booming confidence isn't quite there when ladies are around. "I'm just shy, especially when it comes to girls," he confessed to *Live & Kicking.* "It's true. My confidence drops really low. I've got two different moods—loud and quiet. When I'm really quiet, I just can't approach women. Even if I'm told some girl fancies me, I can't make the first move." But, surely, as a member of a touring band he must have female groupies following him all around. "I'm not into that. I've only ever had long-term relationships," he said.

The reason for this is because J enjoys getting to know a girl, from what sort of things she enjoys doing, to what her opinions are, to what they have in common. J has a soft side to him and knows how to treat a lady. "A perfect date is somewhere quite quiet, somewhere I can get to know the person," he explained to *Teen Beat* magazine. "So, some nice restaurant where you can have a nice meal and conversation and see where it goes from there. I've never understood the going to the cinema part because you can't really talk."

Type he goes for: "All sorts! But I particularly like dark-haired women, not too much makeup and, preferably, a bit older than me." J's also gone on record as saying he loves a girl with a good sense of humor.

Celebrity crush: Kelly Brookes, a fashion model.

Telling quote: "I'm still waiting to do something mad for love."

J is, in many ways, a typical Gemini. True to his sign, this June 13 birthday guy is talented, versatile, smart, and charming. Geminis are usually analytical and easily adaptable to almost any situation. However, Geminis are not perfect by a long shot. The symbol of this sign is twins for a reason. Often Geminis can have a split personality. J himself can attest to this. "Like a true Gemini, I have loads of different sides. I can be the life and soul of the party and then, the next minute, really quiet." On the romantic front,

Geminis are generally drawn to people who are at least as intelligent and attractive as they perceive themselves to be. Once in relationships they tend to be great companions.

Ritchie

Ritchie is soft spoken, polite, and about as pretty as a boy can be. He's also talented, creative, intelligent, sensitive, charming, and at least a hundred more wonderful adjectives, but, in the interest of space, we'll leave it at that. Ritchie is single at the moment, but he has a girl in mind, or at least a very good idea of what she'll be like, when he meets the right one.

"As a person, I like them to be quiet and confident," he confessed to *Teen Beat* magazine. "They can be loud, but they can also chill out. I like them to be stable and happy as people and they have to put family first." She'd better be a smart cookie too. "I like people who can think, people who can talk about the universe and what it's all about," he added.

So, what does she look like, Ritchie? "I'd be

lying if I said looks aren't anything. There has to be a physical attraction straight away. I like them to be able to dress up, but also, when they're at home, be relaxed and have their hair up." Gee, that helps. Actually, Ritchie has said that he imagines his dream girl looks like a cross between Michelle Pfeiffer and Cameron Diaz. Perhaps Ritchie could make a film about it entitled *There's Something About Catwoman.*

Type he goes for: "I used to tend to go
    toward blonds, but now I'm not so picky—
    it's more about if I see something in them,"
    he told *All-Stars* magazine.
Celebrity crush: Cameron Diaz
Telling quote: "Love is really good, but it also
    hurts loads," Ritchie told *Bop* magazine.
    "You know it really hurts, and if you don't
    understand that, you aren't in love."

Born on August 23, Ritchie is dynamic and inspirational, two of the most common traits of a Leo. If Ritchie fits some of the other qualities of his sign, then he may also be generous, energetic, proud, and determined. On the downside, Leos are sometimes a bit vain. In relationships, Leos are passionate, supportive, and protective. However, they are quite particular when it comes to settling on a mate.

Scott

With his changing hair styles and rapid-fire sense of humor, nineteen-year-old Scott Robinson would be one heck of a fun guy to go out with. Of course, it doesn't hurt that he has a beautiful voice to listen to and steel blue eyes to gaze into. But has he got a girlfriend? "I had one when I joined the band, but not anymore," he told *Live & Kicking* magazine. "All the fans are convinced I'm seeing someone, but I haven't been, honest!"

This is not due to lack of interest by any means. Scott loves girls and they love him. It's just a matter of finding the time in his hectic schedule to meet the right girl. When he does, she'll be the envy of all her friends. Scott's more than just brash and funny, he has a sensitive side too. That's right. Don't forget, the guy grew up with two sisters, so he knows a thing or two about ladies.

Scott also fancies himself a romantic, often listening to love songs. "I will be writing my own love songs and I'll be singing them with passion," he revealed in *Bop* magazine. Scott's ideal woman isn't too pushy but isn't a pushover either. "She has to be nice to me and agree to go out with me," he told *Teen Beat* magazine. Scott says lips and eyes are the most important physical feature about a girl. She's out there somewhere, and deep down, Scott knows the right person is worth the wait because "love is special."

Type he goes for: Blond, blue eyes
Celebrity crush: Alicia Silverstone
Telling quote: "I've always wanted to have a girl who likes me for *me*," Scott told *Smash Hits* magazine. "I think the only way I can do that—'cause I don't trust many people now— is to go out with someone I knew before."

Scott's a Scorpio, born November 22. Scorpio may be the most complex of all zodiac signs and there are two distinct types of people who fall under it—positive and negative. Since negative Scorpios are fairly uncommon and we know Scott's a nice guy, let's assume he's positive. If this is indeed the case, Scott is lucky because positive sign Scorpios are believed to be the most richly endowed of all. They are extremely insightful, intelligent, strong-willed people with a remarkable magnetism. On the other hand, Scorpios tend to be a bit arrogant.

When it comes to relationships, Scorpios desire mutual admiration. Typically, the male Scorpio is loving, tender, supportive, and intensely loyal, though, at times, jealous. In fact, Scott admitted to *Live & Kicking* magazine, "I've been quite jealous with girlfriends in the past. I'd always be checking where they were going. One of my old girlfriends used to meet up with her ex and that used to drive me crazy."

Sean

He may be the youngest and shiest member of Five, but that doesn't mean Sean doesn't like girls. In fact, he adores them and makes no bones about admitting it either. On his fact sheet he lists girls as one of his hobbies, as well as one of his five favorite things. The only reason he doesn't have a girlfriend, he says, is because "We just don't have the time to meet any."

Some day soon, Sean will sweep a young girl off her feet. Of course you could fall in love with this lad for his voice alone, but he also has the face of an angel. The British teen magazines say Sean's lips are snoggable (kissable). Behind those big brown eyes lies a sweet, sensitive boy and a romantic one too. Back in school, Sean once saved up his school dinner money every day to buy a girl a present.

A *Teen Beat* magazine reporter asked Sean what his idea of a perfect date was and he said, "I've got too many ideas. Getting to know somebody really well and becoming close. Being somewhere quiet, miles away from noise and people." Sean likes girls who "care a lot and are faithful, and stand by you whatever."

Type he goes for: Girls with class, or, as he puts it, "Girls who don't fart, burp, or drink from a pint glass."
Celebrity crush: Meg Ryan
Telling quote: "I'm emotional and shy."

Born May 20, Sean is a Taurus. If he's true to his sign, then Sean is honest, loyal, gentle, patient, and a great listener. A typical Taurus is a determined worker who is creative, yet practical and organized. However, people born under this sign are not perfect. Stubbornness is the most common trait of the Taurus, hence the term "stubborn bull." Many a Taurus will argue their point until the sun goes down before they'll admit to being wrong. Another common trait of the Taurus is that they can get very jealous. When it comes to matters of the heart, a male Taurus is likely to seek out an attractive girl who will remain loyal and faithful above all else. In relationships, a Taurus generally makes a reliable partner, however he can be a bit possessive.

Okay, you've examined the facts and weighed all your options. So, who's your dream boyfriend? Is it J, Abs, Ritchie, Sean, or Scott? In the end, the decision is an easy one because you can't go wrong. Just be sure and prepare your parents in advance by telling them that the next guy you bring home might have spikey hair or a big tattoo on his arm!

13
numerology

Fans of Five may agree that they are the number one band in the world. And on the love chart, they all rate a perfect ten. But, in numerology, Abs is a nine and J is a one, while Ritchie is a five, Scott is a three, and Sean is an eight. The numerology system was developed by the Babylonians in ancient times. Numerology is a method of determining someone's personality type based on the number of letters in their full name. It's a simple way to figure out what personality type you are. Numerology can also be used for family members, friends, classmates, or, in this case, hot popsters.

After using the method on the Five guys, it was determined that all five band members have different numbers. Does this mean they can't get along? No, just as with zodiac signs, certain numerology numbers are compatible with others. Okay, so Abs has the highest number—this doesn't mean that Abs is the best (though, some of you may feel this way), but it does mean that he gets along well with others—a good thing considering these guys are together practically 24/7! Try it out on your name to see how compatible you are with the Five boys.

Here's what to do. Write out your full name (including middle name, if you have one), and match up the letters with the following chart as with the Five guys examples here.

1	2	3	4	5	6	7	8	9
A	B	C	D	E	F	G	H	I
J	K	L	M	N	O	P	Q	R
S	T	U	V	W	X	Y	Z	

RICHARD ABIDIN BREEN
9938194 129495 29555

JASON PAUL BROWN
11165 7133 29655

RICHARD NEVILLE
9938194 5549335

SCOTT JAMES TIM ROBINSON
13622 11451 294 96295165

SEAN KIERAN CONLON
1515 295915 365365

Next, add up all of the corresponding numbers. You should come up with 99 for Abs, 55 for J, 77 for Ritchie, 84 for Scott, and 71 for Sean. The final step in the equation is to add the two numbers together until you get a single digit. With Abs, for example, $9 + 9 = 18$, and then $1 + 8 = 9$. This makes Abs a nine. Do likewise for J, Ritchie, Scott, and Sean and you come up with a one, five, three, and eight, respectively.

What does this say about the five guys? It says they're a perfect fit. Since all of their numbers are compatible, and there are no obvious conflicts, they form quite a cohesive unit. It's no surprise they are good friends as well as band mates, too.

Are you compatible with J, Sean, or Scott? Do your numbers add up to five or nine, like Ritchie or Abs? Figure it out. See where they fit in and then figure out your number to see if you could be the sixth member of Five. (Would the band then have to add one to its name?) Here are the trait descriptions for the numbers one through nine.

Ones are natural born leaders. They generally keep things organized, but often take on too much work for themselves. Ones thrive on attention, but they sometimes forget to share it and others find them to be a bit selfish. But not everyone. After all, everybody needs friends. That's where numbers two and eight come in!

Twos make good friends, but also good foes. If your best gal pal's a two she'll record all your favorite shows for you while you're on your family vacation. On the flip-side, if you've got any enemies who are twos, guess who'll be the first to spread a rumor about you at school? Twos are also hard workers and patient teachers. Twos match up well with ones, fours, sixes, and sevens.

Always looking for adventure or a good laugh? You must be a **three**. Sociable, energetic, and adventurous are the best way to describe a three. Threes have two weaknesses—they sometimes procrastinate and they tend to be spendthrifts. Threes are compatible with everyone except sevens and twos.

Fours are responsible and trustworthy, but sometimes this makes them a little dull. On the surface they are quite likable, but because fours sometimes don't have much of a sense of humor, they have trouble making friends. But that never seems to bother other fours and eights.

Fives are kind-hearted people, in a broad sense. In other words, a five might spend all of their free time doing volunteer work for worthy causes, yet not realize that a dear friend really needs them. Fives tend to ride a strong wave of emotions with their inner feelings constantly changing with their environment. Sevens, nines, and threes all make good pals.

Sixes are naive and sometimes a bit immature too. For this reason they are sometimes taken advantage of. Sixes also have a rep for getting involved in other people's personal matters. On the bright side, sixes are often upbeat, even when the chips are down. Other sixes, nines, and twos all appreciate that.

A personality type **seven** is a unique person who is a creative thinker. Typically, they are tireless workers who feel like, once they set their mind to a project, they'll stop at nothing to do the best job possible. If this means working overtime or making sacrifices, then so be it! Sevens can be a bit anti-social however. Sevens are very compatible with other sevens, as well as ones, threes, and nines.

The most quiet and reserved of all the numbers is **eight**. However, they have plenty to say when they are around people they know well. For this reason, they make great companions. Eights usually save judgments about others until they've walked ten miles in the other person's shoes. On the downside, eights can be hypersensitive at times and they sometimes don't take to constructive criticism well. Nevertheless, there are plenty of other eights and ones out there for them to hang out with.

Nines are rather complicated folks. On the one hand, they can blend in in just about any situation and can easily get along with just about anyone. They are usually rather charming as well. On the other hand, they tend to turn inward at times, paying so much mind to their own feelings that they neglect others. Nines get on well with everyone except other nines and sixes.

14

five fans unite!

Thanks to Five's devoted record company and management team, as well as modern technology, there are many ways you can get info on Five or contact Scott, Ritchie, J, Sean, and Abs. If you're looking for the latest information about Five, head to your newsstand and check out *Smash Hits*, *Live & Kicking*, *Big!*, *Top of the Pops*, and *Sugar* in Europe; and *Teen Beat*, *16*, *Bop*, *Tiger Beat*, and others in America. For more information, updates and gossip, or a chance to meet other fans, hop online and surf the Internet. There's tons of Five stuff to be found online, including websites, E-mail, and chat rooms.

If, on the other hand, you're like Sean and wouldn't know how to work a mouse, much less log on to a web page, there's always the old-fashioned way. Five has a fan club address, as well as record company and management addresses where you can send fan letters, cards, and gifts—J likes cologne, Ritchie favors teddy bears, Sean prefers T-shirts, and Abs goes for hats, while Scott opts for candy.

Thanks to his well-informed fans, J says he has a bottle of nearly every aftershave on the market. Meanwhile, the Five guys have amassed enough stuffed animals to open a fake zoo. Ritchie has a teddy bear named Benson that one fan gave him before Christmas. It "lives" on his bed.

Who gets the most fan mail? "It's different all over the world," Scott explained to *Superstars* magazine. "J and Sean are very popular in Japan, and in England me and Rich and Abs are quite popular. But fan mail gets split in different ways. J gets mail from the older women, like the moms and the aunts and even the grandparents. I get the younger girls, and so do Rich and Abs. Sean, for some reason, gets a lot of older women as well."

During downtime in their hotel rooms, the guys are as likely to respond to fan letters or E-mails as they are to play Nintendo. Abs especially likes to check out the Info Superhighway. In fact, once while in London he logged onto a Five chat and announced, "Hello, this is Abs," only no one believed him. Scott, J, and Ritchie also go online and often respond to E-mails. Sean, of course, finds it all a bit too modern for his tastes.

A few things to remember:

1. Don't believe everything you read on amateur websites. Since most websites are posted by fans, and not Five insiders, there are bound to be mistakes and misprints. For instance, several websites list J's birth date as 1979, when it's actually 1976. Chat rooms are a fun way to talk with other fans and swap stories about concerts and the like. However, really bad rumors tend to surface in chat rooms, partly because people who don't like the subject of the chat tend to contribute outrageous comments just to be funny. According to some chats, Scott is dating Nicky Appleton from All Saints, J beat up Taylor Hanson, Ritchie is quitting the group to take up modeling, Abs ran off to New Zealand to elope with his girlfriend, and Sean lied about his age—he's really the *oldest* member of the group.

2. If you want to mail a fan letter to Five, be creative. Your letter won't exactly be the only piece of mail the guys will receive that week. Five gets huge sacks of fan mail (thousands of letters per week) sent to their fan club and record companies every day. Use your imagination to make your package stand out from the rest of the pile. On the outside, think big, bold, and bright with colorful envelopes and packages. Inside, grab their attention with a poem, drawing, song lyrics, or something personal like a birthday card.

3. Be patient. Don't expect an immediate response from Five. With so much traveling, rehearsing, performing, and interviewing, the Five guys barely find time for sleep these days. "We get a lot of fan mail now," Ritchie told *Teen Beat* magazine. "I do try and answer personally, but there's so much, my mom answers some for me now." Five adores their fans and will do their best to read and respond to as much fan mail as possible, but until they get a break, it may take time.

4. You may not receive a personalized letter. J, Sean, Abs, Ritchie, and Scott get about a half mil-

lion letters a month from all over the world, plus thousands of E-mails and website hits. At this rate, the guys would have to write thousands of responses every day just to keep up, and then they wouldn't have any time left for making music.

Official Fan Club: Five Club
Lightwater, GU18 5RA,
UK

Record Companies: c/o Arista Records
6 W. 57th St.
New York, NY 10019

c/o BMG/RCA Records
Bedford House
#69-79 Fulham High St.
London, SW6 3JW, UK

c/o BMG Entertainment
International
Carl Bertelsmann Str. 270
D-33311, Gütersloh,
Germany

Via Internet

Official Website:
http://www.bmg-backstage.co.uk
Surf over here for member bios, background info, news, tour dates, and fan club information. You can also check out dozens of other artists on the Arista or BMG record label, like Whitney Houston, Monica, and Gary Barlow, to name a few.

E-mail Address:
5ive@bmg-backstage.co.uk

Unofficial Websites:
There are over a hundred Five websites created by fans from all around the world. Many feature photos, bio data, faves, background information, song lyrics, and, of course, rumors. For a complete listing, use a search engine, like InfoSeek, GoTo.com, Yahoo, Excite, or Lycos. For a composite search of the entire world wide web, try Dogpile. To avoid confusion, narrow your search to entertainment/music/artists.

If you're determined to check out every last site (you'd have to have a whole lot of leisure time), also try different spellings, like "5ive" and "5," but you're bound to come up with a lot of listings for random things since the band's name is also a number, a dollar bill, and a hand gesture. To save you some time, here are a few of the best unofficial Five websites.

High Five—The Unofficial Five Website
http://Five.home.ml.org
Using this URL, you'll wind up at the most comprehensive, fact-filled Five site on the web. *High Five* has over 20 links, including News Flash, Vital Stats, Listening Booth, Photo Album, Field Reports, and much more. A Five fanatic could easily spend hours here.

Five
http://www.geocities.com/sunsetstrip/Towers/6416
Don't let the unoriginal name fool you. This site gives you a look at Five concert pics from around the world.

T-One's Funky 5ive Fortress
http://www.geocities.com/Heartland/Park/4293
A good quality fan site worth checking out. In
addition to some helpful Five facts, you'll also
find links to Aaron Carter, Backstreet Boys,
and Code Red web pages.

Absolut 5ive
http://welcome.to/Five
Welcome to Five's world. This is a terrific site
that features quotes, lyrics, a photo gallery,
games, links, and even a Five screen saver that
you can download. The only problem is that it's
a bit slow to boot up.

KillarSpydar's 5ive Paradise
http://www.geocities.com/Tokyo/Fuji/1941
This fan site from Japan features news and gossip, bios, music, lyrics, pictures, and schedules.

Planet 5ive
http://www.angelfire.com/me/Planet5ive
A fan site from Singapore. Boy, Five really
does have fans all over the place!

Hipper's Webpage
http://www.angelfire.com/tn/hipper/index.html
This site has links to official and unofficial sites for Five, 'N Sync, and BSB. There's also E-mail, a bulletin board, and a chat room link so you can swap info with other Five fans any way you choose.

Merchandise

Five merchandise is now available to fans. Items include T-shirts, posters, key chains, hats, stickers, and more. For a full merchandise catalog, send a self-addressed envelope to the following address:

Five Merchandise Network Ltd.
PO Box 10
London, SW19, UK

15

pop quiz

Okay, you've read the book, you've read the magazine articles, checked out the websites, and listened to the CD a thousand times. Time for a Five pop quiz! Let's find out how much you know about Abs, J, Ritchie, Sean, and Scott. Sharpen your pencil, clear your mind, and answer every last question, but remember, no peeking! When you're finished, check out the scoring section on page 175 to see how you fared.

1. Who is the youngest member of Five?
2. Who is the oldest?
3. Which Five guy has had some rather unusual hair styles?
4. Who's the only band member with a girlfriend?
5. Which guy is called Posh by his band mates?
6. What are the names of the two men who brought Five together at an audition?

7. In what British town have the Five guys lived together?

8. What was Five's first European single?

9. What was their first American single?

10. What is their international record label?

11. Which Five song has a video that features a paint fight in a prep school?

12. Which video takes place in a bowling alley?

13. Which Five track features Scott and Ritchie in a duet?

14. From which song does the line "Do you wanna get down? Do you wanna get funky?" come from?

15. Who is the executive producer for Five who passed away?

16. Who is the famous song writer who previously wrote for Backstreet Boys and 'N Sync and penned several songs on *Five*?

17. What song does the lyric "Five will make you feel all right" come from?

18. Which Five guy is the shyest?

19. Who is the most outspoken?

20. Who is most likely to cry at a movie?

21. Who says he has mood swings?

22. Who is a class clown?
23. What soft drink company signed Five on for an endorsement deal?
24. Which Five guy is an only child?
25. Who went to the same acting school as Emma "Baby Spice" Bunton?
26. Who is Sean's best friend?
27. Who originally made famous the guitar riff from "Everybody Get Up"?
28. What late rap artist does J admire?
29. On which of the following TV shows did Five *not* appear?: (A) *The Ricki Lake Show* (B) *The Jenny Jones Show* (C) *Roseanne* (D) *The Daily Show*
30. At which of the following events did Five *not* perform?: (A) *MTV Live* (B) *Seventeen's* New Star Showcase (C) *Saturday Night Live* (D) Nickelodeon's Big Help
31. Who said this: "Sometimes I feel like Daddy Five"?
32. Which Five guy has two middle names?
33. Which guy doesn't have any?
34. What British TV show is Abs' girlfriend on?
35. True or False: Abs earned his nickname

because he has rock hard stomach muscles.

36. Which two Five pals vacationed together in Greece?

37. Which Five guy got spotted while on vacation in Thailand with his family?

38. Who absolutely hates anchovies?

39. True or False: Five co-wrote most of the songs on their debut album?

40. What week-long tour did Five headline in Great Britain at the end of 1998?

41. Who got their butt pinched during an autograph signing in New York?

42. Which Five guy said he doesn't like New York City?

43. What pop star did Abs idolize as a kid?

44. Which Five guy can't stop eating junk food?

45. Which guy used to be a body builder?

46. Whose mom has a scrapbook of articles written about Five?

47. What activity does Sean take part in in the long form video?

48. Which Five guy goes skydiving in *Five: Inside*?

49. Who gets their shorts pulled down in the video?

50. What activity does Abs take part in during the video?

Answers to the Five Pop Quiz

1. Sean Conlon
2. J Brown
3. Scott Robinson
4. Abs Breen
5. Ritchie Neville
6. Chris and Bob Herbert
7. Surrey
8. "Slam Dunk (Da Funk)"
9. "When The Lights Go Out"
10. BMG/RCA
11. "Everybody Get Up"
12. "When The Lights Go Out"
13. "Until The Time Is Through"
14. "Slam Dunk (Da Funk)"
15. Denniz Pop
16. Max Martin
17. "Got the Feelin'"
18. Sean
19. J
20. Ritchie

21. Abs
22. Scott
23. Pepsi Cola
24. Abs
25. Scott
26. J
27. Joan Jett
28. Tupac Shakur
29. D
30. C
31. J
32. Scott
33. Ritchie
34. *EastEnders*
35. False. It's short for his middle name, Abidin.
36. J and Sean
37. Ritchie
38. Abs
39. True
40. The *Smash Hits* tour
41. Ritchie
42. Sean
43. Michael Jackson

44. Scott
45. J
46. Scott
47. Rugby
48. J
49. Scott
50. Auto racing

Scoring

Compare your answers with the correct ones and add up your total number of right answers. Then check the score groupings below to see how clever a Five fan you are.

38–50 correct: Five's "got the feelin'" you know all there is to know about them.

25–37 correct: It's a "slam dunk." You're definitely down with Five.

15–22 correct: You may listen to Five even after "the lights go out," but you've got a lot to learn about Ritchie, Abs, Sean, Scott, and J.

10–14 correct: "It's all over." Hop online and cruise some Five websites and grab hold of some teen mags. Hey, "it's the things you do" to get to know all about a great band.

0–9 correct: You can't be "satisfied" with a score like this. Come on, Sean is the oldest member of the group and Scott has no sense of humor?! "That's what you told me."

About the Author

Matt Netter works and lives in New York City. He is the author of several other entertainment biographies, including *'N Sync: Tearin' Up the Charts, Backstreet Boys ★ Aaron Carter* and the *New York Times* best-seller *Zac Hanson: Totally Zac!* He's currently scouting out the next great pop group.

DON'T MISS ANY OF OUR
BEST-SELLING POP MUSIC BIOS!

2070

Dancin' with Hanson

Make sure you have the real stories of Hanson, told for the first time by Ravi, the guitarist who toured with the brothers during their incredible year at the top.

Packed with all the backstage info on Taylor, Isaac and Zac, exclusive behind-the-scenes photos, and Hanson memorabilia, this scrapbook is a must-have for every true Hanson fan!

RAVI

Available in April 1999

From Archway Paperbacks
Published by Pocket Books

What's it like to be a Witch?

Sabrina
The Teenage Witch

"I'm 16, I'm a Witch, and I still have to go to school?"

●●●●●

Based on the hit TV series
Look for a new title every other month.

From Archway Paperbacks
Published by Pocket Books   1345-08

"Well, we could grind our enemies into powder with a
sledgehammer, but gosh, we did that last night."
— XANDER

BUFFY
THE VAMPIRE
SLAYER™

As long as there have been vampires, there has been
the Slayer. One girl in all the world, to find them where
they gather and to stop the spread of their evil ... the
swell of their numbers.

#1 THE HARVEST

#2 HALLOWEEN RAIN

#3 COYOTE MOON

#4 NIGHT OF THE LIVING RERUN

THE ANGEL CHRONICLES, VOL. 1

BLOODED

THE WATCHER'S GUIDE
(The Totally Pointy Guide for the Ultimate Fan!)

THE ANGEL CHRONICLES, VOL. 2

Based on the hit TV series created by Joss Whedon

 Published by Pocket Books

1399-08